Colourful Characters of Cumbria's Eden Valley

Colourful Characters of Cumbria's Eden Valley

John Sharpe

HAYLOFT PUBLISHING LTD
CUMBRIA

First published by Hayloft 2015

Hayloft Publishing Ltd, South Stainmore,
Kirkby Stephen, Cumbria, CA17 4DJ

tel: 017683 41568
email: books@hayloft.eu
web: www.hayloft.eu

Copyright © John Sharpe, 2015

John Sharpe has asserted his right to be identified
as the Author of this Work

ISBN 978 1 910237 08 3

This book is sold subject to the condition that it shall not, by way
of trade or otherwise, be lent, resold, hired out, or otherwise
circulated without the publisher's prior consent in any form of
binding or cover other than that in which is is published and
without a similar condition incuding this condition being imposed
on the subsequent purchaser.

A CIP catalogue record for this book is available
from the British Library

Papers used by Hayloft are natural, recyclable products made from
wood grown in sustainable forests. The manufacturing processes
conform to the environmental regulations of the country of origin.

Designed, printed and bound in the EU

Frontispiece, Joseph Scott, Penrith, who became 'Mr Los Angeles'

Contents

Acknowledgements   7
Preface   9
Foreword   11

1   Philip, Duke of Wharton in Westmorland (1698-1731)   13
      Pampered young aristocrat who squandered a vast fortune

2   John ('Jack') Robinson, MP (1727-1802)   16
      Wily Westmorland politician with influence in high places

3   James Lowther, 1st Earl of Lonsdale (1736-1802)   18
      Ruthless aristrocrat commonly known as 'Wicked Jimmy'

4   Revd. William Warkman (1744-1811)   29
      Long-serving chaplain to Northumberland's dashing Delavals

5   John Metcalfe Carleton (1753-1829)   43
      York-born Old Etonian rake of the Eden Valley

6   David (1797-1855) and William (1799-1876) Workman   51
      Sons of a country family who pioneered the American West

7   Anthony Trollope (1815-82) at Penrith   59
      World-famous novelist who invented the Post Office pillar-box

8   Henry Bloom Noble (1816-1903)   63
      The Isle of Man's greatest benefactor

9   Captain John Noble (1825-61) and the *Tayleur*   69
      White Star ship sank on its maiden voyage with great loss of life

10   James Barker Bland (1854-1942)   74
     Footloose farmer with intellectual interests

11   William John Woodhouse (1866-1937)   78
     Railwayman's son who became a professor of Greek in Australia

12   Joseph Scott, 'Mr Los Angeles' (1867-1958)   81
     Penrith-born emigrant to fame and fortune in California, USA

13   Washington Family in Westmorland   102
     And the Virginian who nearly went to Appleby Grammar School

14   The 'Peacracker' Lives on   105
     The search for a veteran motorcycle

About the Author   110

Acknowledgements

These portraits have all appeared in one form or another as articles in the *Cumberland and Westmorland Herald,* and I am grateful to the newspaper's editor for general permission to reproduce those articles in various other publications such as newsletters of historical societies.

The underlying facts in each case are the product of original research wherever possible, in preference to less reliable secondary sources such as the internet (even if the internet held any information of apparent value on any of these figures – which was rarely the case). This general rule holds true even if it entailed appreciable travel to, and occasional correspondence with, repositories in Cumbria and much farther afield.

In particular, my thanks are due to:

Cumbria County Archives at Kendal, Carlisle and Whitehaven
Sedbergh School Library
The Metcalfe Society
Northumbria County Archives at Gosforth and Alnwick
Durham Diocesan Archives
Ushaw College Library, Durham
York Castle Museum
Liverpool Maritime Museum
Manx Museum in Douglas, Isle of Man
Missouri Historical Society, St Louis, Missouri, USA
Taos County Historical Society, Taos, New Mexico, USA
Kit Carson Home and Museum, Taos, New Mexico, USA
Workman Family Homestead Museum, Los Angeles, California
City Library, Los Angeles, California, USA

Original inspiration for a series of portrayals of local characters came from the late John Hurst, editor of the *Cumberland and Westmorland Herald.* Other individuals who come to mind as being especially helpful and encouraging throughout the long history of this biographical project include

Colourful Characters of Cumbria's Eden Valley

the Los Angeles Workman Museum's assistant manager Paul Spitzzeri, retired Liverpool surgeon and maritime historian Sam Davidson, retired engineer and Workman/Warkman family historian Charles Atkinson of Niagara Falls, Ontario, and the late Frank Goodfellow, long-serving churchwarden at Earsdon near Newcastle-upon-Tyne.

John Sharpe
Clifton, Penrith, Cumbria

Preface

For some years John Sharpe has been publishing articles on Cumbrian history and biography in the *Cumberland and Westmorland Herald*. Readers of these popular pieces and John's many fans in local history groups who continue to enjoy his well-chosen and lively talks will now welcome the publication of his collected essays.

Colourful Characters of Cumbria's Eden Valley is the product of many years of exhaustive research in more than a dozen archives in this country and the United States. And yet the deep learning is lightly worn, producing vivid vignettes written in a lively, reader-friendly style, while the political and economic background is carefully filled in. Perhaps it is as a result of his many years of police service that John loves a villain – mad, bad and dangerous to know – such as the rakish Philip, Duke of Wharton, or James Lowther, first Earl of Lonsdale, a 'madman, too powerful to be confined'; the madcap prankster Sir Francis Delaval seems to spring straight out of the pages of *Blandings Castle*.

Families as well as individuals are well represented in these studies – all those children so tragically lost before their time! Lowthers keep popping up of course, members of that larger-than-life dynasty with their base near John's beloved Clifton. Yet though John Sharpe's focus is local his range is far from introverted. Above all, 'Professor Clifton' establishes the Eden Valley as a nursery of America: the wild-westerner Kit Carson puts in an appearance as an associate of the Workman brothers of Clifton, and a Workman granddaughter is an early star of the silver screen. John Sharpe's study of the Penrith-born Joseph Scott, 'Mr Los Angeles', is the definitive biography of that remarkable Cumbrian migrant.

Here then is an attractively produced and well illustrated volume by an expert who knows how to make scholarship popular.

Michael A. A. Mullett,
Emeritus Professor of History,
University of Lancaster.

Colourful Characters of Cumbria's Eden Valley

Foreword

The Eden Valley sounds idyllic. But what about the people who have made it what it is? What about the people who left it far behind yet never forgot the place? Why do the valley's place names appear on memorials to the great and good in Northumbria and the Isle of Man – and even in California and Australia? How is it that people of the valley have made their mark half way round the world, without ever forgetting their family origins in the old English counties of Cumberland and Westmorland?

Lady Anne Clifford, the fifth Earl of Lonsdale ('the Yellow Earl') and William Wordsworth get all the attention from the biographers and students of Eden's high-profile personalities. But what about the 'most extraordinary' Duke of Wharton, the first Earl of Lonsdale ('Wicked Jimmy') and old-Etonian squire John Metcalfe Carleton of Helbeck, Brough? What do we know about characters like them? What do we know about leading Victorian novelist Anthony Trollope's connection with Penrith?

Why does the Noble name appear so often in the Isle of Man? Why does the Workman name – once so common in the Eden Valley – show up so much in Los Angeles of all places, along with roads like Clifton Street and Penrith Drive? Why does LA's Grand Avenue have a statue of Abraham Lincoln alongside a figure immortalised in bronze who turns out to be from Penrith? Does Appleby-in-Westmorland really have a connection with President George Washington? Is it true that Georgian Prime Minister William Pitt the Younger was once Appleby's MP?

This book is founded on the notion that we do not always know as much as we might about our area's most important asset – its people. It does not pretend to be an historical treatise or a work of reference but rather a journalistic compilation of portrayals of some extraordinary characters associated with Cumbria's Eden Valley, often with a quick look at their ancestry. The tone is light-hearted where possible but never intentionally frivolous and always respectful where respect is due.

Sums of money are mentioned throughout the book, some of them huge for their day though appearing quite small now. Giving today's equivalent value is not easy. The early twenty-first century equivalent of £1 in 1750 or 1850 depends on what one wants to buy, what is available, and relative costs at the time. Prices did not rise much in the nineteenth century, but twentieth century inflation caused prices to rise some fifty-fold, so that what would have cost £1 in 1914 would now mean spending around £50.

To give an example of salaries, in the 1750s the annual pay of a Captain in the Royal Navy was around £150; a curate received about £30-£40 per annum; and a lower rank domestic servant could expect about £4-£5 a year plus board and lodging.

Philip, Duke of Wharton in Westmorland
Pampered young aristocrat who squandered a vast fortune

Raised to the highest rank of the peerage before his twentieth birthday, Philip Wharton was "the most extraordinary creation of an English dukedom on record" *(Dictionary of National Biography)*. A ruthless ambition inherited from warrior forebears at their Eden riverside stronghold near Kirkby Stephen was matched in Duke Philip by a rebellious spirit fired up by youthful exposure to the eighteenth century fleshpots of Europe.

Sir Thomas Wharton had done the family proud when Henry VIII made him a baron for routing the Scots on Solway Moss in 1542 and sacking Dumfries. His successor at Wharton Hall was in the thick of Border strife, and flamboyant barons three and four were equally adept at picking the right side in troubled times.

Thomas Wharton, the future fifth baron, married the decidedly plain but fabulously wealthy heiress Anne Lee, before neglecting her for his horses and proceeding to establish an enviable reputation as England's greatest rake. Affairs of state were wily Thomas's *milieu* as well, and he was a leading light in the movement to replace Catholic King James II with Protestant William of Orange. William and Mary had just been proclaimed joint sovereigns in 1689 when Thomas was appointed a Privy Counsellor and Comptroller of the Household, before succeeding to the peerage with a massive income on the death of his father and going on to be Viscount Winchendon and Earl of Wharton. A two-year stint as Lord Lieutenant of Ireland earned him a nice set of Irish titles for 'rooting out popery', and advancement to Marquis of Wharton came just before his death in 1715.

In the meantime, Thomas had lost his long-suffering first wife and married even richer heiress Lucy Loftus. Their only son Philip was born just before Christmas 1698 and baptised on 5th January 1699, when the fabulously favoured infant's godparents were King William III and Princess (later Queen) Anne, no less.

Young Philip showed remarkable scholastic promise but was just sixteen when he shattered his doting father's hopes of family aggrandisement with a prudent alliance, by eloping with an impecunious army officer's daughter (and soon deserting her). Both his parents died soon afterwards and sixteen-year-old Philip by inheritance became 2nd Marquis of Wharton and 2nd Marquis of Malmesbury.

The precocious marquis set off for Geneva to learn strict Protestant principles like his father but soon tired of that idea and ran into debt when he exceeded the generous allowance made by his trustees. He met the Pretender 'James III' in Avignon less than a year after the 1715 Jacobite uprising and went on to Paris to see the British ambassador, who counselled him on the dangers of associating with the Pretender. Philip responded by drinking the Pretender's health and smashing the ambassador's windows as he left.

Before leaving France, the artful aristocrat extracted the then enormous sum of £2,000 from Maria Beatrice, widow of the exiled King James II, on the pretext that the money would be used to promote the Jacobite cause in England.

Heading next for Ireland, where his late father had excelled at 'rooting out popery', Philip took his seat in the House of Peers as the Marquis of Catherlough and distinguished himself in debate by his zeal for the anti-Catholic government, before drawing up a congratulatory address to George I on "a happy increase in the royal family." His Protestant credentials thus established, he had just turned nineteen when he was created Duke of Wharton in Westmorland on 28th January 1718.

Entering the English House of Lords on his 21st birthday, Duke Philip soon exercised his considerable talents as an orator with so vitriolic an attack on the Stanhope government's integrity that Lord Stanhope had an apoplectic fit and died the next day.

While Philip was denouncing vice in high places, his reputation for high jinks won him the presidency of Sir Francis Dashwood's 'anything goes' Hell Fire Club. When the king issued a proclamation to suppress the notorious body, Philip produced an old family bible in the Lords and quoted a few well chosen texts to show he was no patron of blasphemy.

Not even the vast estate Duke Philip had inherited could sustain his life of dissipation, and the Wharton properties in Yorkshire, Westmorland, Oxfordshire and Buckinghamshire went to trustees for the benefit of his creditors. The Westmorland estates were sold in 1730 to Robert Lowther of Maulds Meaburn.

But Philip had long since left for Vienna, where he announced his conversion to Catholicism and openly adopted the cause of Pretender 'James III'. Moving on to Madrid, he treated with ostentatious contempt an order to return to England and busied himself with an elaborate project to restore the Pretender to the English throne. Even worse, he served as a Spanish volunteer at the siege of Gibraltar in 1727, for which he was outlawed by resolution of the House of Lords and indicted for high treason.

Repairing to Paris, Duke Philip sought solace with the disgraced Jacobite Bishop of Rochester, but his long-suffering trustees in England were ordered to cut off his funds and his next three years were spent wandering about western Europe in a state of drunkenness and beggary, pursued by a clamouring mob of creditors. His health broke down and he died in a Spanish monastery on 31st May 1731, aged 32.

John ('Jack') Robinson, MP
Wily Westmorland politician with influence in high places

Captain John Wordsworth's body was found on a Dorset beach on 20 March 1805, six weeks after the good ship *Earl of Abergavenny* went down in a storm off Portland Bill. That a Wordsworth had commanded the pride of the East India Company's fleet since its launch at Harwich in 1796 was down to the Member of Parliament for that ancient Essex port who had influence aplenty with the noble Earl of Abergavenny himself – and was a wily Westmerian to boot.

John Robinson, MP, was born at Appleby-in-Westmorland on 14 August 1727 and educated at the town's grammar school, before being articled to his lawyer uncle Richard Wordsworth of Sockbridge near Penrith, grandfather of Captain John Wordsworth and the poet William.

Town clerk of Appleby by 1750 and mayor in 1760, John Robinson inherited much property from his grandfather and married the daughter of a wealthy Barbados merchant, soon buying the Cockermouth mansion that would become known as Wordsworth House and rebuilding the imposing White House in Appleby.

Still in his early 30s, "steady, sober-minded, industrious, a clever man of business," John Robinson became principal law agent and land steward to the all-powerful Sir James Lowther, later first Earl of Lonsdale, who made him a magistrate and deputy lieutenant for Westmorland before nominating him as the county's member of parliament in 1764.

Sir James expected his nine parliamentary nominees to obey him on all matters of policy, but in 1774 John Robinson, by now Secretary to the Treasury in Lord North's administration, incurred his ruthless mentor's wrath by disagreeing with him over the deepening crisis in America. John declined Lowther's challenge to a duel – the great man's usual redress in such circumstances – but had to resign as his law agent and find himself another seat in the House of Commons.

John Robinson represented Harwich from October 1774, and settled in Isleworth, Middlesex. Accustomed to attacks by Whig opponents in the

Commons, on one occasion he heard Richard Brinsley Sheridan, MP, complaining of bribery to silence opposition to government policy amid shouts of "Name, name!" Sheridan stared across at John Robinson on the Treasury bench and conferred on him an immortality of sorts by exclaiming: "Yes, I could name him as soon as I could say Jack Robinson!"

Offered a peerage by George III in 1784, John Robinson declined because he had no son but ventured to ask His Majesty to promote his daughter Mary's father-in-law instead, and the 15th Baron Abergavenny duly became first Earl. The earl died a year later and was succeeded by his son, the Hon Henry Neville, Recorder of Harwich and John Robinson's son-in-law, thus making the former Mary Robinson a Countess. John Robinson died at Harwich in 1802 and was buried at Isleworth near his daughter Mary, Countess of Abergavenny, who had died six years earlier.

This son of Appleby had been a consummate London politician, but fate was not so kind to his Sockbridge cousin and protégé, John Wordsworth, who became a Lowther law agent and moved with his new wife, formerly Anne Cookson of Penrith, into the Cockermouth mansion later known as Wordsworth House, where their five children would be born, most notably William in 1770, and John two years later.

John and Anne Wordsworth were both dead by 1783 and funds were desperately low, for poor John had never been paid his due in all the years he had served the Lowther cause – although generous benefactors who sent young William and John to Hawkshead Grammar School saw the budding poet go up to Cambridge while John went off to sea.

When the 1,500-ton *Earl of Abergavenny* put to sea at Harwich in 1796, it was named after John Robinson's son-in-law Henry, the second earl, and the ship's captain was another John Wordsworth, Whitehaven cousin of the ill-fated Cockermouth family – and of John Robinson. Young John of Cockermouth joined the crew, and a meteoric rise through the ranks took him to the captain's cabin before he was 29 in 1801.

On 5 February 1805 the 400 souls aboard the *Earl of Abergavenny* were barely out of Portsmouth bound for Bengal and China when their mammoth voyage ended in stormy seas off Portland Bill with the loss of 260 lives, and Captain John Wordsworth went down with his ship. His brother William, sister Dorothy and sister-in-law Mary were consumed by "miserable affliction" when the shocking news reached them a week later at Dove Cottage, Grasmere.

James Lowther, First Earl of Lonsdale
Ruthless aristocrat commonly known as 'Wicked Jimmy'

'Wicked Jimmy' was the scornful nickname that stuck when James Lowther, first Earl of Lonsdale, died at Lowther Hall in 1802. Corrupt electioneering had been his forté, but his claims to notoriety were rooted in many other fields as well for he was a ruthless autocrat and a heartless egotist with no regard for countless unfortunates who crossed his tyrannical path.

For over eight hundred years the Lowthers – members of Parliament, knights, baronets, Viscounts and Earls of Lonsdale – have had their base at Lowther in the old English county of Westmorland. By the mid-eighteenth century the Lowthers had become the largest landowners and the most politically powerful family in the north-west, with branches in Yorkshire, Lancashire, Ireland and London. Sir Hugh Lowther was King Edward I's Attorney in 1291 and an MP in 1305, and in every succeeding generation Lowthers have been people of importance and often of distinction, including 58 MPs and thirteen members of the House of Lords.

Three Lowthers accompanied Henry V to Agincourt in 1415 and another received Mary, Queen of Scots, on her flight to England in 1568. A Lowther risked his life and property in support of William III during the revolution of 1688, before serving in his cabinet. Successive Lowthers developed the town, port and collieries of Whitehaven, and our subject in this case was unequalled in the eighteenth century art of corrupt electioneering. More recent Lowthers include a friend and patron of the poet William Wordsworth, the larger-than-life sportsman known as The Yellow Earl, and a distinguished Speaker of the House of Commons.

Born at Maulds Meaburn Hall on 5 August 1736, James Lowther was the eldest surviving son and heir of Robert Lowther and his wife Katherine, only daughter of Sir Joseph Pennington of Muncaster Castle in Cumberland and his wife Margaret, formerly Lowther.

Robert Lowther's father, Richard, had inherited Maulds Meaburn Hall, ten miles from Lowther, on the death of his father in 1675. Richard married

Barbara Prickett of Wresal Castle in Yorkshire in 1679 and Robert was their eldest surviving son. On 14 August 1704 at Poplar in London, he was 22 years of age when he married widow Joan Carleton. She was in her forties and had been born in Barbados, where her grandfather had settled in the 1650s. Joan had seen two well-to-do Barbados husbands die within a decade, when she married Robert Carleton from Penrith. In his forties, Robert Carleton was sound in body and mind when he made his will in November 1702 and was dead within a year, leaving all he had to his "dear and loving wife Joan," who made Robert Lowther her fourth husband a few months later.

The enterprising lady had come into a fair bit of property from those three childless marriages, including Robert Carleton's mansion house at Penrith and a sugar plantation at Christchurch in Barbados with mansion house, still house, rum house, forty cottages, stables and horses, cattle and four hundred and twelve slaves (more or less, according to Robert Carleton's will). She and new husband Robert were very comfortably off when they married in London that summer's day in 1704.

Robert Lowther, MP for Westmorland from 1705 to 1708, was in the House on 23 October 1707 when it became the Parliament of Great Britain on the Union of the Crowns of England and Scotland. In 1708 he was appointed to the Ordnance Board at £400 a year. Two years later and still just 28 years of age, he became "Captain-general and Governor-in-chief of Barbados, St Lucia, Dominica, St Vincent and the rest of the Caribbean Islands lying to windward of Guadeloupe in America."

Robert Lowther landed at Bridgetown with his Barbados-born wife Joan and her sister Barbara in 1711, to find he had taken on a tough job for his £2,000 a year salary, for Barbados had long been a hard place to govern. English settlers had arrived in 1627, and most of the inhabitants now resented control from England, many of them being ardent Jacobites.

After a string of complaints against Governor Lowther, he was recalled by Queen Anne in February 1714 but managed to convince her of his own competence and integrity, insisting that he had been the victim of a Jacobite plot to secure the islands for the Stuart cause. In November 1714, three months after Queen Anne's death, Robert was re-appointed Governor by George I and was back in Bridgetown six months later.

After another five years as Governor of Barbados amid continuing controversy and complaints of corruption, oppression and arbitrary conduct, Robert returned to England in 1720, where his wife Joan died two years

Colourful Characters of Cumbria's Eden Valley

James Lowther, First Earl of Lonsdale

later. The busy sugar plantation continued to give him a tidy income, and he divided his time between London and Maulds Meaburn. In 1730 he paid £26,000 for the Westmorland estates of the last Duke of Wharton, who had been convicted of high treason and deprived of his property. This included all the lands of the former Shap Abbey.

The Governor, as he was known for the rest of his life, was a widower until 22 June 1731, when at the age of 49 he married 19-year-old Katherine Pennington, his first cousin twice removed. By the time Robert died aged 63 on 13 September 1745 – of a heart attack said to have been brought on by the Jacobite uprising – they had six children.

Son James was seven when his elder brother Henry died in 1743. He went to school initially in Marylebone, London, but eventually attended a Hertfordshire boarding-school where bullying was rife – and he was a victim until he was big enough to do the bullying himself. James went up to Peterhouse, Cambridge, at the age of sixteen but left a year later.

James was nine years old when his father died in 1745, leaving property in Westmorland and Barbados, and just fourteen when he inherited his great-uncle Henry's Lowther baronetcy with vast estates in Westmorland, before coming into the family's industrial empire at Whitehaven in 1755 with around £2 million and the Yorkshire estates the year after that.

Said to be 'the richest commoner in England' before he came of age, James was already being schooled in ruthless ambition by his widowed mother Katherine. An intelligent and forceful woman, she kept a watchful eye on her favourite son's interests and was determined that he would make the most of his wealth and position. She had a willing pupil.

Sir James Lowther first entered parliament in 1757, for Cumberland, and eventually controlled nine seats, a tally that was second only to the Duke of Newcastle with eleven. Seven seats were in the north and two at Haslemere in Surrey, collectively known as 'Lowther's Ninepins' – because his MPs had to follow his political line on all issues, otherwise they had to go. Lord Lieutenant of both Westmorland and Cumberland by his early twenties, in 1761 he married Lady Mary Stuart, daughter of the 3rd Earl of Bute. The match was hardly made in heaven but it was good for his social status without curtailing his amorous adventures.

Sir James Lowther's political heyday was well before the nineteenth century Reform Acts started to shake up a system of representation in parliament that had remained unchanged for centuries, certainly not democratic

---

Opposite, the will, dated 1702, of Robert Carleton of Penrith, (1656-1703)

in any modern sense of the term and with no concept of universal suffrage or regard for changes in distribution of population.

The House of Commons in 1780 had 558 members, two from each of the forty counties – usually country gentlemen from long-established local families – and most of the rest from the 200-odd cities and boroughs which also returned two members each but were still based on the wealth and prominence of the towns in medieval times. Entitlement to vote varied enormously, sometimes being limited to a town's corporation or freemen and sometimes to the owners of properties or 'burgages'.

A well-off individual could control a borough by instructing the voters, bribing the corporation or simply owning the burgages. Landowners would often tell their tenants how to vote, and voters could sell themselves to the highest bidder. Meals and alcohol were standard forms of bribery, and in 1761 a Gloucester MP complained that two voters had been murdered, having been plied with so much brandy that they had suffocated with a very fat man in the confined space of a post chaise.

Most boroughs could be purchased for around £3,000 or £4,000 by leading political families. Constituencies varied wildly in population between old but small towns such as Appleby and Haslemere, returning their two MPs as they had always done, and bigger but newer urban areas that were not boroughs so not represented in parliament other than by their county members. Even towns like Leeds, Birmingham, and Manchester in the eighteenth century had no MP of their own.

Cumberland and Westmorland counties each had two parliamentary seats, with around 4,000 freeholder electors in Cumberland and 2,000 in Westmorland, and the three local boroughs were Carlisle, Cockermouth and Appleby. At Appleby and Cockermouth the voters were owners of plots of land called burgages – around 250 at Appleby and 280 at Cockermouth – and whoever owned most of them could simply nominate his MP. Carlisle was a Freeman Borough with around 700 freemen out of a population of about 7,000. The most notorious of all nineteenth century 'rotten boroughs' was Old Sarum in Wiltshire, which still returned two members of parliament even though no one had lived there for centuries.

Sir James Lowther's political master-stroke came at the general election of 1780, when he nominated a 21-year-old London barrister for his vacant seat at Appleby. The young man (who had never been to Appleby) took his seat in January 1781 and soon became even better known than Sir James himself, as William Pitt the Younger, Chancellor of the Exchequer in 1782

James Lowther, First Earl of Lonsdale

and Prime Minister in December 1783 at the age of twenty-four. Sir James was elevated to the peerage as the first Earl of Lonsdale within months and showered with viscountcies and baronies to boot.

The so-called 'mushroom election' at Carlisle in 1786 was targeted by the new Earl for a Lowther relative. Just 700 city freemen had the vote, so he arranged to create 1,400 honorary freemen ('mushroom voters') who were Whitehaven miners, local militiamen and subservient tenants from elsewhere in the county. This swung the outcome in Lowther favour, and a political cartoonist had a field day with a caricature of triumphant clown John Lowther prancing off along Corruption Lane to Westminster while the earl himself took an axe to the Tree of Liberty with his legs astride the River Eden and his feet among 1,400 mushrooms. Wicked Jimmy was above the law.

The then Recorder of Carlisle was also a Lonsdale nominee – James Boswell, biographer of Dr Johnson, lawyer of modest ability and incorrigible rake, who thought currying favour with the all-powerful earl might help his own political ambitions. Lampooned by the *Cumberland Pacquet* for stupidity and impudence, 'Bozzie's' uneasy association with Wicked Jimmy ended in a row a few months later when his lordship threatened to "put a bullet in Boswell's belly." A violent temper was the first Earl's most noticeable attribute, and a challenge to a duel was his favoured method of silencing anyone with the temerity to oppose him.

The noble gentleman's legendary adroitness in the political sphere was matched by his capacity for merciless parsimony. Mining subsidence at Whitehaven in 1791 caused an inrush of water which drowned three workers and five horses below ground in the Duke Street area and damaged properties elsewhere in the town. Henry Littledale, a mercer of Somerset House, sued the Earl of Lonsdale at Carlisle Assizes, and the Earl reacted by closing his Whitehaven mines until he received 2,500 signatures on a petition begging him to reopen them and promising to indemnify him against all such actions in the future.

Sockbridge-born John Wordsworth, lawyer, father of the poet William, and Sir James Lowther's agent at Cockermouth, was owed nearly £5,000 in unpaid fees when he died aged 42 in 1783, and the indigent Wordsworth family's protracted legal action for redress was fruitless. William had been eight years of age when his mother died and thirteen when he lost his father; childhood experience of financial hardship due to aristocratic meanness left its mark in a rebellious spirit that even made him an early admirer of revolutionary France.

Less well known is the sad case of Daniel Bloom, an educated young Londoner who came north in 1766 to manage the Lowther carpet factory. Housed in the solid grey building that is now the Lowther Estates office at Lowther Newtown, the carpet factory had a history dating back to 1680, when the then Sir John Lowther, later Viscount Lonsdale, decided to enlarge the old Lowther Hall that had been his family's seat for generations. The grand new house would have stood in the middle of the old village, and his lordship's solution to the amenity problem was to shift the village a few hundred yards to the east.

Among the new buildings that collectively became known as the village of Lowther Newtown was a 'manufactory' for linen and carpets. In 1697 textiles were abandoned, and the large building then became a school. Lowther College was intended for the sons of gentlemen, and it soon showed promise. In 1700 Robert Molesworth (later Viscount Molesworth) thought the college would be suitable for his four sons. Sir Joseph Pennington of Muncaster sent his son there in the 1720s and recommended it to Sir John Penicuik, the Scottish coal magnate.

In 1731 Sir John visited his son George at Lowther College, finding it to be "a large building containing two great halls and twenty-two rooms for the scholars," who were paying £12 a year for board while being educated in Greek and Latin in preparation for university. Headmaster from 1715 was William Wilkinson (1685-1751), a native of Crosby Ravensworth and graduate of Queen's College, Oxford. The college closed when Wilkinson left in 1740 to become vicar of Lazonby, and the building then reverted to its former role as a factory.

The then viscount's idea in restoring the site to its original purpose was "to promote a spirit of industry among his poor tenants, and getting them better bread than they would otherwise have had; and that with very little or no loss to their benefactor." Run by a William Bramwell with a system of outworkers in the villages between Clifton and Bolton, by 1746 the mill was showing a healthy profit of more than £151 per year. Flax was grown locally and also imported, and linen products were being sent as far afield as Whitehaven, Liverpool and Newcastle.

With the death of the third viscount in 1751, there began the long reign of the young Sir James. In 1752 Mr Bramwell submitted a detailed report to 'Madam' (Sir James's formidable widowed mother, Katherine) on his operations at the manufactory since his lordship's death the year before. The report met with the lady's approval and the mill stayed in business.

In due course the young Sir James, starting to earn his place in the family annals as the notorious 'Wicked Jimmy', got a grip of things himself, particularly after his mother's death in 1764. Not the sort to have any truck with his predecessor's ideas like better bread for his poor tenants, he was not going to be anybody's benefactor except his own.

In London Sir James met one Daniel Bloom, a well educated man of obvious business acumen. Then in his late twenties and recently married at fashionable St Martin's-in-the-Fields, Daniel by 1766 was running the manufactory at Lowther. Having got the management of the mill on a more professional footing with Daniel Bloom, James turned his attention to the operatives. Like the well-bred students who had been housed on the site in its days as a school, the workers who would produce the high-quality floor coverings would be young people – but of a quite different breed from the affluent youngsters who had pored over their Latin verbs.

Sir James called at the Hospital for the Maintenance and Education of Deserted Young Children in July 1772 and signed up for the release to himself of four girls aged twelve to fourteen as apprentices. Clearly pleased with this first small batch of foundling children, Sir James collected another fifteen girls a few months later. In March 1774 he signed for another half-dozen children – including three little boys this time, aged nine to eleven. The 25 impressive indentures – each signed *James Lowther* in his own bold style – indicated that two of the ten-year-olds were to be employed in household business while the others were destined for the carpet factory.

Now lodged at Lowther in rural Westmorland, the unfortunate children presumably were a long way from where they had been abandoned, and some of their names had a pathetically ironic ring about them – names like Catherine Silver, Blanche Orchard, Temperance Reel and Patience Rutland. In 1787 Daniel Bloom still had one of the girls from the first batch of foundlings collected by Sir James in 1772, now nearly 30 years of age. By this time, incidentally, Daniel and his long-suffering wife had a daughter of their own, Mary aged eleven. She was to be their only child: as things had turned out at Sir James Lowther's carpet factory, perhaps they felt they were already looking after everyone else's children.

After years of financial hardship Daniel finally found the courage to appeal in writing to his autocratic and utterly impervious employer for money to support his wife and family and run the factory. Deep in debt, he had never been paid his due and had been keeping the orphan factory workers largely out of his own pocket for 25 years, "which has quite Beggar'd us." Dated 19 September 1797, the desperately obsequious letter was put on file with no record of a response.

James Lowther, first Earl of Lonsdale, died on 24 May 1802 of a "mortification of the bowels," according to *The Times*. He bestrode the counties of Cumberland and Westmorland like a colossus for half a century, yet it is difficult to find anything positive to say about him: he truly was "a madman, too powerful to be confined." If a family needs a black sheep, then Wicked Jimmy laid unassailable claim to that role in his family. It was left to his successor, Sir William Lowther of Swillington (later 1st Earl of the second creation), to repay with interest the long-standing debt to the Wordsworth family, and he was good to the long-suffering carpet factory manager Daniel Bloom and his wife Mary in their retirement at Eamont Bridge.

The worst problem the first earl left to his successor was arguably Lowther Hall itself. Not long after it was rebuilt amid such upheaval in the 1690s, it had burned down and stood a partial ruin for decades while the first viscount's successors like Wicked Jimmy continued to live in one of the fire-blackened wings. It seems the miserly earl may have thought about rebuilding as early as 1760, but he never got round to it and it was not until the early years of the nineteenth century that architect Sir Robert Smirke got to work on creating the enormous castle that would be the Lowther family's grandiose home for over a hundred years.

James Lowther, First Earl of Lonsdale

Sir James Lowther, first Earl of Lonsdale (1736-1802), 'Wicked Jimmy'.

The first Earl of Lonsdale was a man of immense wealth and political influence who spent enormous sums on elections and lawsuits. More than £60,000 worth of gold was said to have been found in his home at Lowther after his death. By his will of 1798, his wife had the house and furniture at Fulham, among other things, while his sisters got over £60,000 with the Barbados estate of £4,000 a year. The Yorkshire estate of £5,000 a year was devised to Mr John Lowther, and those in Cumberland and Westmorland (supposed to be worth £40,000 a year) went to Viscount Lowther, with about £100,000 in personal estate.

The ladies who lurk in the shadows of Wicked Jimmy's murky life include a Miss Lowes in the 1770s and a mysterious Mrs Tabberer later on, but doubtless there were more.

Reverend William Warkman
Long-serving chaplain to Northumberland's dashing Delavals

'THE Right Honourable John Lord Delaval, Baron Delaval of Delaval in the county of Northumberland, and Susanna Elizabeth Knight, spinster, both of this parish, were married in this Church by licence this 5th day of July, 1803, by me (signed) *Wm Warkman, Curate and Minister.*'

The brief entry in the register of the ancient St Alban's parish church at industrial Earsdon, near Newcastle-upon-Tyne, was made by an enterprising man of the cloth who had been ministering for 35 years to parishioners who were very different from the agricultural folk of his old home village in Westmorland.

William Warkman was born at Brownhow Farm, Clifton, near Penrith, and baptised at the village church on 8 July 1744, the third son of yeoman farmer Thomas Warkman and his wife Anne. He was probably educated at the prestigious Appleby Grammar School, leaving home for Newcastle at the age of nineteen with a £30 legacy when his eldest brother inherited the long-held family farm, and was still just 24 when he became vicar of Earsdon on 25 September 1768.

Coal miners' humble dwellings were everywhere about Revd. William's Earsdon. But within sight of his little hilltop church was Seaton Delaval Hall, the palatial residence of the aristocratic Delavals, with its Norman chapel which had been consecrated by Bishop Flambard of Durham in the year 1102, and which the young cleric was required to attend "whenever the Delaval family desired his assistance."

The wealthy Delavals could boast an unbroken lineage going back to the time of William the Conqueror; and Admiral George Delaval spared no expense when he commissioned playwright-turned-architect Sir John Vanbrugh to design his new mansion in 1717 – although he did not live to see it finished in all its baroque splendour for he died in a fall from his horse in 1723.

The admiral's nephew, Captain Francis Delaval, RN, inherited the estate, and he was succeeded in 1752 by his son, Sir Francis Delaval MP. The dashing Sir Francis entertained on a lavish scale both at Seaton Delaval and in London, once even borrowing Drury Lane Theatre for his own production of *Othello* while the House of Commons adjourned two hours early to be present. A consummate practical joker, he was fond of pranks like dousing his house guests with cold water in the middle of the night and pulling aside partitions of their rooms to reveal an embarrassed occupant in a state of undress.

When Sir Francis died aged 44 in 1771, the Rev William Warkman officiated at the funeral, and Sir John Delaval, Bt, himself quite an extrovert who was no stranger to the revelries at Seaton Delaval and in London, succeeded his older brother as head of the family.

Sir John was in dire need of William Warkman's ministrations on 7 July 1775, when his only son and heir, nineteen-year-old John, died at the hands (or rather a well-aimed foot) of a spirited laundry maid to whom the amorous young aristocrat was 'paying his addresses.' Seaton Delaval mourned again when Lady Susanna, Sir John's wife of 35 years, died on 1st October 1783, just a few months before the politically astute baronet was raised to the peerage as the first Baron Delaval.

William Warkman and his wife Elizabeth by this time had a family of eleven children at Earsdon, but they still found room at the vicarage for William's adventurous young nephew Thomas, who had left an unhappy home at Clifton in Westmorland while still a teenager.

Such, though, was the Revd. William's standing with Lord Delaval that in 1796 he became rector of Ford, an idyllic rural domain of his lordship's in the north of the county, while still retaining the living of the coal-mining parish of Earsdon. It was natural that when his lordship remarried at Earsdon at the age of 75 in 1803 – to a local woman less than half his age – the ever-attentive Revd. William would be in charge of the ceremony.

John, Lord Delaval, died on 17 May 1808, joining his first wife in the family vault in London's Westminster Abbey. His old friend and confidant Revd. William Warkman was called to higher service at Ford three years later, having enjoyed the patronage of the 'gay Delavals' for nearly 43 years.

William was succeeded at Earsdon by his youngest son Henry, MA of St Andrews, who was destined to be vicar of Earsdon for 46 years until his death at the age of 74 on 12 March 1857. Among the many achievements of Henry's long ministry was his success in 1837 in having a new church of St Alban built on the site of the 'ruinous' old one.

However, in later life Henry's income was less than £100 a year for

The 1814 Warkman Chalice.

serving a busy parish of 11,000 people. Like his father before him, he regularly attended Seaton Delaval chapel, three miles away, with the lament, "I am obliged to walk, as I cannot keep a horse. I have eight children, and have been obliged to bring up my sons as mechanics."

Before leaving the Revds William and Henry Warkman to rest in peace, it is worth recalling that the village of Clifton, the former's birthplace in Westmorland, achieved its claim to fame on 18 December 1745 with the Battle of Clifton Moor, the last time two armies clashed on English soil, while Ford had already won its place in history with its proximity to the scene of the terrible Battle of Flodden Field on 9 September 1513.

The parish of Earsdon staked its claim to fame in perhaps even more poignant fashion on 16 January 1862. At 11am that day the most terrible calamity that had ever visited any coal mine in Britain occurred at New Hartley Pit near Seaton Delaval, when the 42-ton cast-iron beam of a pumping engine broke in two and half of it fell down the pit shaft, taking tons of debris with it. The impenetrable mass of rubbish completely blocked the only means of exit from the pit, and 204 miners perished in the workings 420 feet below the surface.

The bodies of the victims, some only ten years of age, were recovered a week later, and their mass funeral took place at Earsdon church on 26 January 1862. A memorial was later erected in St Alban's churchyard.

The Revds. William and Henry Warkman, father and son, between them served the parish of Earsdon and the Delavals for nearly 90 years. But the Warkman story that began at the old family farm at Clifton in the Eden Valley did not end at Earsdon or Ford in Northumberland. "Brought up as mechanics" Henry's sons may have been, but some of them showed all the adventurous spirit of their illustrious grandfather – and more, with travels that took them to North America and Australia.

Revd. Henry acknowledged his late father's Westmorland origins when in 1838 he named his sixth and last son Thomas Clifton Warkman. In 1861, as a 23-year-old ship's engineer living with his three unmarried sisters in Elswick, Newcastle-upon-Tyne, Thomas was just about to launch himself on a remarkable sea-faring career that would take him all over the Mediterranean and across the Atlantic.

Thomas Clifton Warkman was in Trieste in 1865 when he married Guiseppina Trombetti from Bologna, and they soon started a family of twelve children (of whom only four survived to adulthood) whose registrations of birth would chart their parents' movements around the seaports of Italy and France. Thomas Clifton Warkman was in New York several times in the 1880s, sailing from European ports such as Messina, Palermo and Liverpool, and in 1889 he was joined in New York by his Italian wife Guiseppina and two of their children, from Palermo in Sicily. Tragically, Thomas Clifton was killed in a steamship explosion in Brooklyn Harbour, New York, early in 1893, leaving his widow Josephine, as she was now calling herself, to move around various addresses in the city until her death there in 1909.

The three highest-profile offspring of Thomas Clifton, senior, and Guiseppina (later Josephine) Warkman were their three sons – Thomas Clifton who was born in Venice in 1870, then Henry and Richard Clifton,

Lowther Castle – nineteenth century Lowther family seat near Penrith, (photograph Peter Koronka)

Colourful Characters of Cumbria's Eden Valley

Memorial to the 204 victims of the 1862 mining disaster at New Hartley Pit.

Colourful Characters of Cumbria's Eden Valley

St Martin-in-the-Fields where the funeral of John Metcalfe Carleton's father took place on 2 August 1788. The church was completed in 1726, and the first church warden was King George I, the only reigning monarch to hold such a position. The Royal Box in the church is reserved for the Royal family, with whom St Martin's has always retained a special relationship.

John Metcalfe Carleton rented No. 26, Southampton Street, Covent Garden (just off The Strand) from 1789-1793. It is about five minutes' walk from St Martin-in-the-Fields.

The Red House, Appleby-in-Westmorland– eighteenth century home of Thomas Carleton, (photograph Peter Koronka)

Colourful Characters of Cumbria's Eden Valley

Above, Wordsworth House, Sockbridge, eighteenth century home of the poet's grandfather Richard, (photographs Peter Koronka)
Below, Wharton Hall – Wharton family seat near Kirkby Stephen

Colourful Characters of Cumbria's Eden Valley

Above, the old Lowther carpet factory (now the Lowther Estate Office). Below, the two-bedroom Victorian terrace house in Dodds Street, Darlington was home to the Scott family for many years from the early 1870s. In 1880 Joseph and Mary were living here with seven children aged between 17 and just a few months, including 13-year-old son Joseph. Young Joseph's place of birth in Penrith in 1867 has not been established, but it could have been his grandparents' public house at No. 36 King Street.

The White House, Appleby-in-Westmorland – eighteenth century home of John Robinson, MP, (photograph Peter Koronka)

both born in Marseille, France, in 1876 and 1878 respectively.

Brothers Henry and Richard Clifton Warkman both emigrated to the USA after the tragic death of their father in 1893. In New York in 1893 Henry married a lady of Irish Catholic extraction. Their son Thomas was born in Brooklyn and became a seaman with ports of call such as Panama and Le Havre in France to his credit, before leading a colourful life on the New York waterfront in the prohibition era and then disappearing in mysterious circumstances in Illinois, only to reappear some years later with a different surname. Richard Clifton Warkman was in Virginia in 1918 and became a US citizen in 1943 in Chattanooga, Tennessee, where he died ten years later.

The younger Thomas Clifton Warkman who started life in Venice in 1870 was destined for a remarkable career of travel that took him to New York soon after the death of his father in Brooklyn and ultimately half way round the world. A marine engineer, he served in the United States Navy in the 1898 war with Spain and took part in the Battle of Manila Bay in the Philippines.

Returning to the UK in 1900, Thomas Clifton, junior, became a freemason and married 23-year-old Jessie Wilhelmina Robertson from Edinburgh. Back in the United States via Ellis Island in 1903, by which time he had become a marine surveyor with the Salvage Association of London, he and Jessie moved to the city of Milwaukee in Wisconsin, on the west shore of Lake Michigan some 100 miles north of Chicago. It was there that their three children were born: Julia Ford in 1904, Thomas William (1905) and Henry Earsdon (1909) – thereby preserving in the family the Revd. William Warkman's Christian name and the English placenames associated with their long-gone ancestor's ministry.

The Warkman family lived in Milwaukee from 1903 until 1917. On 6 December 1917 the most terrible marine disaster occurred in the Canadian harbour of Halifax, Nova Scotia, with a collision between two ships loaded with ammunition destined for the First World War battlefields of France. The resulting huge explosion caused great loss of life and much of the town of Halifax was destroyed. Thomas was despatched to the scene of the calamity to carry out surveys and quantify losses, and his commitments there kept him busy, off and on, for the next ten years. He also made frequent trips to the UK during this time.

His wife Jessie and their two surviving children, Thomas William and Henry Earsdon (daughter Julia Ford having died, sadly, about 1909 in Milwaukee) seem to have spent some considerable time in Virginia during the period of Thomas' prolonged absence in Halifax, Nova Scotia. In 1923 Jessie and the two boys were in the UK for around three months.

In 1927 Thomas was transferred to Vancouver, British Columbia, Canada, where he opened an office for the Salvage Association and where he was to remain for the rest of his life – but with frequent trips abroad, such as the visit he and Jessie made in 1930 to Honolulu, Hawaii, returning to Vancouver via San Francisco. Thomas was in Honolulu again just a month later, on his own this time, returning two weeks later via Los Angeles. The following year he made several trips to the wreck of the *SS Columbia* off the coast of Mexico.

Thomas Clifton Warkman continued to cross the Atlantic to the UK in the 1930s, one such trip being from Montreal to Liverpool in 1936, when he probably visited his old home at Earsdon, Northumberland, to make the presentation to the parishioners of the ornate silver chalice which had been awarded in 1814 to his grandfather, Revd. Henry Warkman (and which presumably had been kept since then by family members). The chalice was stolen from St Alban's church in the 1990s and was never recovered.

In 1938, when Thomas Clifton was in his late 60s but had no thoughts of retirement, he travelled – by air this time – from Vancouver to Los Angeles, before going on to Honolulu and then to Manila in the Philippines to assess damage to a ship by fire. It was a sign of the times that he was able to make the return trip from the Philippines by air.

In the late 1930s and early 1940s he remained as busy as ever, travelling widely around the west coast of America and visiting places like Honolulu, Los Angeles and San Francisco. Indeed, he continued to work as a marine surveyor until he died on 14 January 1944 in the American city of Seattle, while on a business trip from his home in Vancouver. His widow Jessie died in Vancouver on 1 December 1959, aged 79.

John Metcalfe Carleton
Old Etonian rake of the Eden Valley

'A spirited but unfortunate gentleman' was Parson and White's cryptic verdict on John Metcalfe Carleton in 1829, and Brough-under-Stainmore's later guide books did nothing to lift the veil on the mysterious Georgian Squire of Helbeck.

Publishing their respected *Directory of Cumberland and Westmorland* coincidentally in the very year of Squire John's demise in far-off Surrey, Messrs Parson and White were surprisingly generous in their allusion to the Old Etonian entrepreneur who had made his mark on the Eden Valley half a century earlier, for the man was really a bit of a scoundrel. In fairness, though, John had greatness thrust upon him at a tender age, despite a troubled childhood, and it was his misfortune to tangle with the ruthless first Earl of Lonsdale, while ample good taste inspired his grand manor house that graces the Helbeck hillside to this day.

St. Michael-le-Belfrey, York.

Perhaps it was ominous that John was baptised (Metcalfe – the Carleton name came later) at the same York church that had seen the baptism of archconspirator Guy Fawkes. Both were in their thirties when they fell from grace, but Squire John lived to tell the tale – and more, for his downfall in Westmorland was followed by a phoenix-like rise from the ashes to lord it over a sumptuous Surrey estate that had been home to a Lord Chief Justice of England and had even received King George III.

The Eden Valley squire was born in York and christened John Metcalfe at the church of St Michael-le-Belfrey, close by the city's Minster, on 1st September 1753, fourth of five children of York lawyer/landowner John Metcalfe and his wife Elizabeth, née Carleton of Appleby. Their marriage at Appleby in 1748 had linked two well-to-do middle class families with their respective origins not far apart in Yorkshire's Wensleydale and Westmorland's Eden Valley; but what seemed on the surface like a sound arrangement sadly would soon all end in tears.

Our subject John was barely two years old when a little brother and sister died and he was still only seven when his parents went their separate ways. Father John repaired alone to his country estate at Bellerby near Leyburn and the old manor house with its loyal housekeeper Mary Brown, leaving his wife in York with her teenage daughter Elizabeth and young son Thomas.

John was sent to Appleby-in-Westmorland to live at the imposing Red House in Boroughgate with his maternal grandfather, wealthy lawyer Thomas Carleton. Without a son and heir, scheming widower Thomas saw in his grandson the prospect of carrying on the long-established Carleton name in the town while keeping his hard-won property empire together – and out of the hands of detested Yorkshireman John Metcalfe, who had gone against his wishes and married his only surviving daughter.

John Metcalfe Carleton would be Master Metcalfe's name from now on, and in 1763 his elderly grandfather drafted a deed purporting to sell the nine-year-old boy all his Westmorland estates for just £100 – to come into effect after his death but inevitably subject to ratification by the manorial courts which at the time had the final say in such matters, before ownership could legally change hands. Then he tucked the document away with his convoluted will and contrived to keep out of the way of being questioned on details of the dubious transaction by officials of the various manorial courts that had jurisdiction in the places concerned.

Thomas Carleton died aged 80 in 1765, but things did not go according to plan. It worked at Clifton near Penrith, where Sir James Lowther's manorial court allowed the wily old lawyer's 1763 deed, and eleven-year-old John Metcalfe otherwise Carleton was enrolled as proprietor of a small farm that had belonged to his late grandfather.

It was a quite different story at the Earl of Thanet's manorial court at Appleby a few months later, when astute court steward Thomas Heelis rejected the late Thomas Carleton's deed of 1763 and instructed the jury to find Carleton's daughter Mrs Elizabeth Metcalfe heir to the properties in question. This Appleby ruling was followed in respect of all the other Thomas Carleton estates in the Eden Valley, and his daughter Elizabeth was enrolled as the new proprietor in each case.

This meant that the properties intended by Thomas Carleton for his grandson went to his married daughter Elizabeth instead, and thus passed automatically to her estranged husband – precisely the outcome Thomas had schemed to avoid. The thorny problem fuelled family friction that persisted for years and kept the lawyers busy until young John finally bought out both his parents' interest in the properties. That was in 1779, the year when John built his enigmatic Fox Tower with its panoramic view over his newly-confirmed estates between Brough and Clifton.

In the meantime, John had left school at Eton and become lord of the manor at his late grandfather's freehold estate at Helbeck, Brough. Still in his early twenties – and not badly off but a lot less affluent than he would have been if his grandfather's property plan had worked – he rebuilt elegant Helbeck Hall and laid out its grounds regardless of expense. But his ambitions far exceeded his bank balance and he was soon beset by some increasingly impatient and vociferous creditors.

Despite the rigours of the Stainmore track to Scotch Corner, and the nine

Helbeck Hall, Brough.

days travel in his coach on the Great North Road that a trip to the capital entailed, John Metcalfe Carleton often indulged his cosmopolitan tastes from the comfort of a rather fine town house he rented at three guineas a week in London's Covent Garden, where an enterprising Georgian gentleman would find the night life somewhat more congenial than it was up in stuffy old Westmorland.

John's travelling expenses on a typical outing from Helbeck to London came to just over £4, the main item being hay and corn for the horses at around four shillings a day – rather more than it cost him for his own three meals and tot of rum. He could have done the 280-mile trip a bit more cheaply and a lot more quickly on the daily Mail Coach which passed through Brough on its way to the capital, but the bumptious squire was not the sort to take readily to the rigours of public transport.

However, beset as he was by the clamouring of his creditors, and constant friction with his parents and his brother Thomas over money, the irrepressible country squire and man-about-town plunged into his most ambitious business venture. Not content with investing heavily in the local lime kilns, lead mines and collieries, his ultimate objective as an entrepreneur was to bring the Industrial Revolution to the upper Eden Valley.

By the stream in wooded Yosgill below Fox Tower (but nicely out of sight of Helbeck Hall) John piled all his dubious capital into the construction of a cotton mill which had 50 workers by the year 1790. The average age of the spinners who did most of the work was around fourteen, although one or two were children as young as six. As one contemporary observer approvingly put it, John's mill was "a great benefit to the poor of Brough, whose children can earn their living at six or seven years of age."

Helbeck products went on sale as far afield as Manchester, the hub of the cotton trade, and also in Glasgow and London. Novice industrialist John Metcalfe Carleton was always in debt, and raising the wherewithal to finance this overblown cotton manufacturing operation had left the reckless squire deeply in hock. For centuries the county of Westmorland had made its fortune on the woollen industry whereas it was not well suited to cotton for various reasons. The reckless squire owed money to some very powerful people, most notably the fabulously wealthy but utterly ruthless Sir James Lowther, lately raised to the peerage as the first Earl of Lonsdale. 'Wicked Jimmy', as his lordship was commonly known to the employees and tenants he held in thrall, was minded in 1789 to demand the return of his capital and interest but had second thoughts, for reasons best known to himself.

In the meantime, John was embroiled as ever in problems with the parents he blamed for his unhappy childhood in York, and his poor mother Elizabeth bore the brunt of his resentment. Petulant John had fared rather better with his less indulgent father, and he got some return for that when his father died at Bellerby manor house in 1788, leaving nothing to his estranged wife Elizabeth. His housekeeper Mary Brown got a house and land and, like her only son John, a useful £30 a year. His son Thomas in York got £50 a year while Squire John of Helbeck was favoured with just £30 a year but appointed executor and residuary legatee of his father's estate.

St Martin-in-the-Fields, London

For executor John there was work to be done, and quickly, since his father had recalled his metropolitan origins with the requirement that his mortal remains be interred in the crypt of the parish church of St Martin-in-the-Fields in London. This proved to be an 18-day mission for the undertakers and cost £226, a hefty bill which, for once, John settled promptly. His dispute with his long-suffering mother over financial arrangements for her went on until she died two years later, leaving everything to her son Thomas, who had stayed with her all along in York.

The insufferable John had brought upon himself constant problems over money matters with his much quieter and more conscientious brother Thomas, as well as with his parents, and their relationship at one point got so bad that the younger man was moved to write to John to say, "I think you use me very ill. I shall be very glad to be on good terms with you: there is only you and me left."

By now a Justice of the Peace for Westmorland, John was busy in London procuring a coat of arms for himself and extracting substantial loans from well-to-do residents of prestigious addresses like Hanover Square and Berkeley Square, while making his Carleton surname official and planning to change his marital status.

Negotiations for the hand of an Essex girl foundered on a dispute with her wealthy father over financial arrangements, and John turned his amorous attention to one Sarah Richardson, originally the daughter of a Brough publican and by now a lonely young London woman whose husband was languishing in the city debtors' prison. Rescued from the horrors of the Poultry Compter by a loan from the devious John – and terrified of the attentions of some very unpleasant creditors who had somehow discovered his subsequent hiding place – the hapless cuckold soon disappeared in mysterious circumstances. John then moved in with the deserted wife and they lived together at some expensive London addresses until their marriage at Southwark in 1799, when the requisite seven-year time lapse allowed Sarah's missing husband to be legally presumed dead.

Meanwhile up at Helbeck, the inevitable had happened, and early in 1793 John, then aged 39, was declared bankrupt with massive debts, by far the biggest creditor being the despotic first Earl of Lonsdale who was owed nearly £1,370. The cotton mill fell silent, the workers lost their jobs and the long process began of selling off everything moveable at Helbeck, until the estate itself came up for auction in London in 1799.

Arrogant as ever and undaunted by a spell in York debtors' prison, which was quite probably instigated by his exasperated brother Thomas, the thick-skinned John cared no more for the inquiries of the Bankruptcy Commission than he did for the distress of his many creditors, secure as he was in the knowledge that he stood to inherit a lot of valuable London area real estate which had belonged to his long-gone paternal grandfather, after expiry of an elderly aunt's life interest in it.

When his aunt, Sarah Metcalfe, the last remaining of three unmarried sisters of his late father, died in 1804, John reluctantly satisfied most of his clamouring creditors and moved into magnificent Kenyon House in Thames-side Richmond, Surrey, whose previous occupant had been Lord Chief Justice Kenyon, a close friend of King George III, who was himself a frequent visitor to the house in the 1790s. Tragically, John's long-suffering wife Sarah, whose health was supposed to have been causing concern, drowned there in the icy water of the ornamental pond one dark night in

John Metcalfe Carleton

The Fox Tower.

early December 1809. John avoided the embarrassment of an inquest but could not keep the shocking occurrence out of the newspapers: *The Times* carried a report about the "old lady of great respectability" who had died at her home in Richmond (Sarah was aged 44).

Surviving the crisis as usual, John found a replacement for poor Sarah in the shape of a younger lady called Ann Dangerfield, who moved in with him at Kenyon House and shared his palatial residence for the next two decades. That they never married would scarcely have raised an eyebrow in the polite society at nineteenth century Richmond.

This was the time of mad King George and the Regency. At Bushy, just over the river from Richmond, was a mansion occupied by a popular actress called Dora Jordan and her numerous offspring. The comely Dora had a total of thirteen children, ten of them by her long-term co-habitee at Bushy who was known by the polite fiction of 'Mr Jordan' but was in fact William, Duke of Clarence, third son of George III and later to be King William IV. A contemporary caricature by cartoonist Gillray portrayed the Duke and Dora in Richmond Park, a touchingly devoted couple, with him, paunchy and sweating, pulling a packed baby carriage like a New Man while she walked happily alongside, learning her lines, the model career woman. (Eventually and inevitably the inimitable Duke of Clarence succumbed to pressure to marry and produce a legitimate heir, so he ditched poor Dora, who died in France in 1816, lonely and hounded by debt collectors).

John Metcalfe Carleton, consummate con-man, irresponsible social climber and archetypal Georgian rake, died at Kenyon House in Richmond on 21 November 1829, and went to his last resting place at St Luke's church in affluent Chelsea. He had no family. His only close relative was his brother Thomas, who died two months later in Ripon, Yorkshire, also without issue. The only other child of the late John and Elizabeth Metcalfe to live beyond infancy was the brothers' elder sister Elizabeth, who had died years earlier in York at the age of 23.

David and William Workman
Sons of a country family who became pioneers of the American West

David Workman and his brother William were amazingly adventurous sons of the old county of Westmorland who took the early American West by storm but never forgot the quiet corner of England where their story began. The Workman family story comes into focus around the year 1640 – but probably began a lot earlier than that – at their Brownhow farm in the rural parish of Clifton near the feudal seat of power at Lowther. In the 1770s, though, the prosperous farm that had fed several generations for at least a century and a half was beset by domestic problems that led to family breakdown and the eventual sale of the property.

Thomas Workman, Brownhow's teenage son and heir, left home and went to live with his clergyman uncle William at the village of Earsdon near Newcastle-upon-Tyne. The Revd William was an educated man who had left Brownhow while still in his teenage years, like young Thomas, and had been ordained in the diocese of Durham while also establishing himself as chaplain to the aristocratic Delaval family of Northumberland.

The all-powerful Delaval connection got courageous young Thomas Workman his first job as an apprentice glazier and also took him south to London, where he met and married one Lucy Cook from Godalming in Surrey. Thomas had been far from his birthplace in Westmorland for almost twenty years when his personal circumstances changed dramatically. Early in 1794 his well-to-do uncle David Harrison, the childless brother of his mother Agnes Workman, died at Clifton and left Thomas his extensive estate in the village.

Hastening north with two small daughters to claim their sizeable inheritance, Thomas and Lucy Workman first made their home at the Westmorland village of Temple Sowerby, before moving with their growing family into the substantial former Harrison family home at nearby Clifton which they were to occupy for the rest of their lives.

Thomas and Lucy Workman's eldest surviving son David was just 21 years of age when he opened this transatlantic drama of pioneering enterprise in 1818 by leaving Clifton for the United States with £100 cash, to set up as a saddler, along with Penrith man John Nanson, at the rough-hewn frontier settlement of Franklin, Missouri.

When Nanson left the partnership two years later and funds ran low, David made the 10,000-mile round trip home to raise more cash and recruit his younger brother William. Back at the saddlery by the Missouri River, the enterprising Workman brothers took on a young apprentice called Kit Carson, whose destiny was the stuff of legend as America's ultimate frontiersman and scout, a man of his time who would give his name to many

David Workman. Photograph by kind permission of Workman family.

The Workman brothers' journey from the UK to the US. Map by Mike Kirchoff, cartographer, Loudon, Tennessee.

William Workman, 1851, in New York when he was en route from California to Clifton. Photograph by kind permission of Thomas E. Temple, Los Angeles.

places in the West like Carson City, capital of the state of Nevada, and become a brigadier-general in the US Army.

With David's runaway apprentice Kit not far behind, William braved the Great Plains of the Cheyenne and the bison in 1825 on the 1,000-mile Santa Fe Trail to Nuevo Mexico, newly free of the crumbling Spanish Empire but still over twenty years from US annexation. He sold illicit 'firewater' in that exotic northern outpost of Mexico west of the Pecos River and took a leading role among shadowy beaver trappers of the Rocky Mountains, the 'reckless breed of men' who were America's original Wild West pioneers. While the Clifton family fretted for news of errant sons so far from home, William survived desperate illness and clashes with Indians to become a naturalized Mexican and set up home with a local senorita and their two children at a place called Taos.

Hidden away at 7,000 feet in the Sangre de Cristo Mountains of New Mexico, Taos (rhymes with 'house') was a scattering of dirt-floored adobe dwellings dominated by the twin towers of a little church, its streets littered with animal dung and the central plaza either dry and dusty or ankle-deep in mud, depending on the season. A chaotic haunt of gun-toting trappers and smugglers, and a magnet for Comanche and Navajo raiding parties, Taos could hardly have been more different from the peaceful old Clifton that William had left just three years earlier.

A hard man who was not always on the right side of the law (such as it was) in tough times, William Workman progressed from trapper to store owner and outfitter of trapping expeditions, and did well for himself in shaky New Mexico. In 1841 he stood accused of siding with the hostile Republic of Texas and plotting to assassinate New Mexico's despotic Governor Manuel Armijo as civil disorder threatened to engulf the troubled territory. It was time to head West once again.

Governor Armijo railed against William's 'torrent of evils' in his volatile domain as the intrepid Englishman was well on his way to leading the first significant settler party 1,200 miles over America's toughest pack-mule route across the blistering Mojave Desert to the little Mexican pueblo de

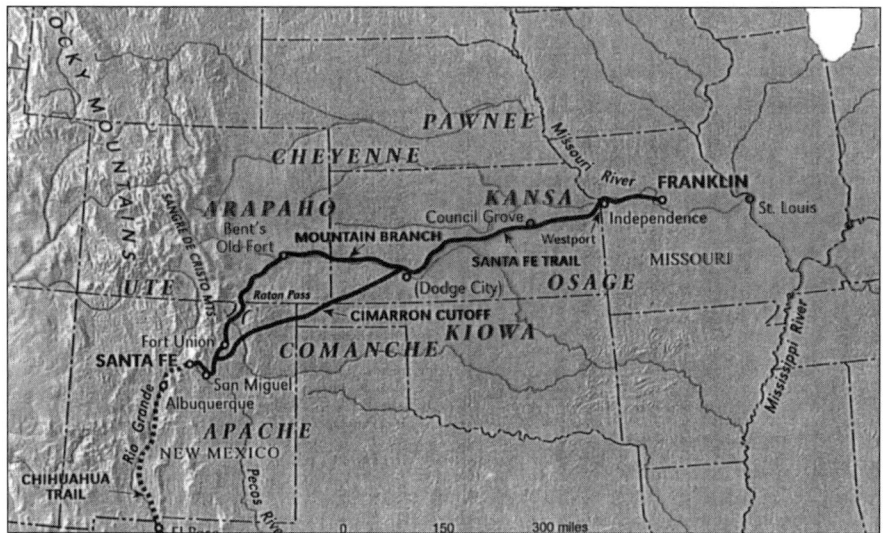

The Santa Fé Trail, William's 1825 pack mule route from Missouri to New Mexico. Map by Mike Kirchoff, cartographer, Loudon, Tennessee.

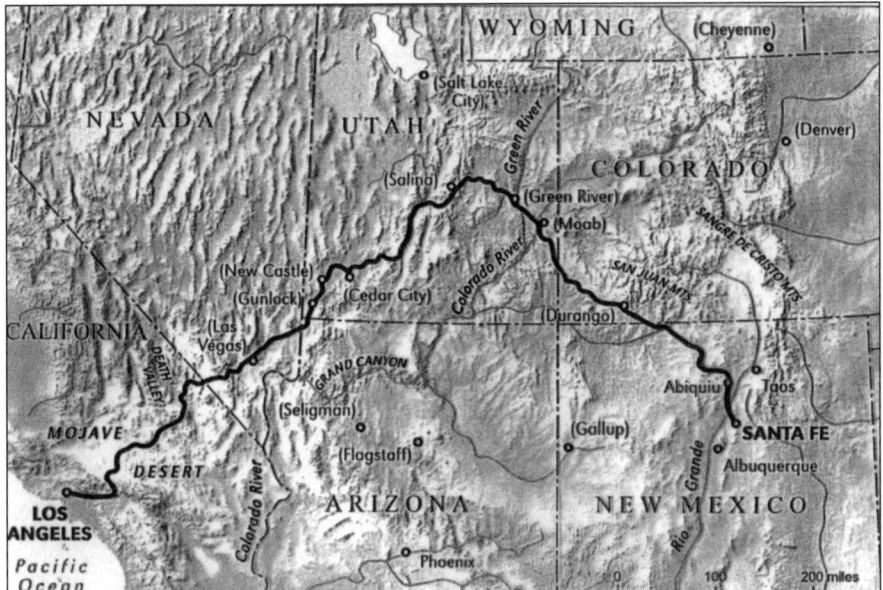

The Old Spanish Trail, William's 1841 pack mule route to America's far West. Map by Mike Kirchoff, cartographer, Loudon, Tennessee.

Los Angeles, where a well-placed $1,000 in gold won him the 18,000 acre Rancho La Puente. Unerring loyalty to California's embattled Governor Pio Pico earned rancher William respect as 'Don Julian', while La Puente grew to nearly 50,000 acres and other real estate came the energetic newcomer's way for services rendered – including even Alcatraz Island in San Francisco Bay.

The US-Mexican War hit fabled California not long after William Workman reached the Pacific shore with his dynamic band of American pioneers. He brokered the surrender of Los Angeles to American forces early in 1847 – just a few days before his old friend Charles Bent, who had stayed on in New Mexico and become the territory's first American civil governor, was shot and scalped by a rebellious mob of Mexicans and Indians in Taos.

Three years later Gold Rush riches sent William on a six-month journey via Acapulco in Mexico and the Gulf port of Vera Cruz to New York and across the Atlantic to London and the home of his youth at Clifton, where he was welcomed by a brother and sister he had not seen for nearly 30 years. London's Great Exhibition opened in May 1851, and this extraordinary traveller was among the six million people who visited the capital for that celebrated event. The year 1851 was well before London got the benefit of

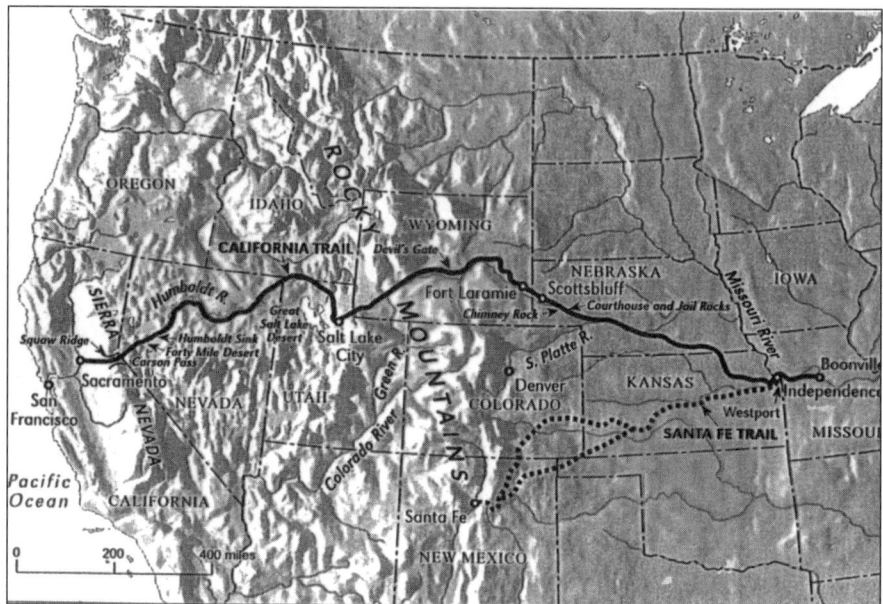

The California Trail, David's 1854 wagon train route from Missouri to the far West. Map by Mike Kirchoff, cartographer, Loudon, Tennessee.

a Victorian sewage system and William, tough as he was, had to get himself a prescription for stomach powders...

Back in California, rancher William prospered as Los Angeles grew from a small Mexican pueblo into a violent cow-town of the 1850s and matured into the American capital of an agricultural empire with a limitless future. In 1868 he and a flamboyant son-in-law founded the growing town's second bank, but a few years later the acclaimed Workman and Temple Bank failed with the loss of his beloved Rancho La Puente and William tragically ended his own life with a gunshot.

When self-assured young William and restless apprentice Kit hit the trail for New Mexico in the 1820s, David Workman stayed on to marry in frontier Missouri but was widowed within a year then flooded out of his riverside home. Rehoused and remarried by his early 30s, he went on to be an inveterate trader over the Chihuahua and California Trails and survived everything from robbery in El Paso to fire in Sacramento and marauding Sioux and Cheyenne on the prairies of Nebraska. As the Plains Indian Wars loomed and Civil War storm clouds gathered over Missouri, he led his family 2,000 miles west by wagon train to Los Angeles and met an untimely end in California's booming goldfields.

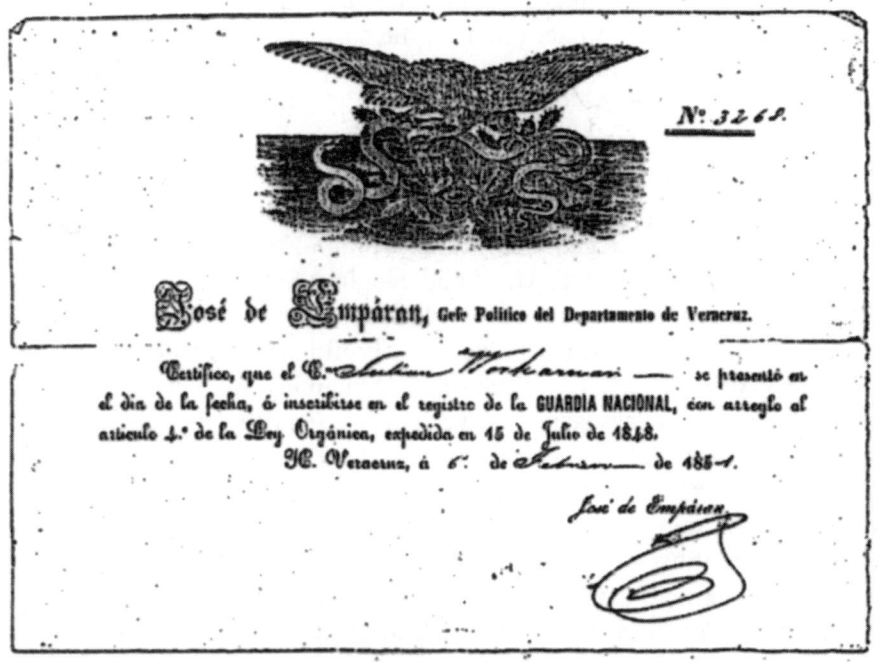

William (aka "Julian") Workman's check-in document at Veracruz, 1851

José de Empáran, Gefe Político del Departamento de Veracruz.
Certifico, que el C. *Julian Workaman* [sic] se presentó en el día de la fecha, á inscribirse en el registro de la Guardia Nacional, con arreglo al articulo 4 º de la Ley Orgánica, expedida en 15 de Julio de 1848.
H. Veracruz, á 6 de Febrero de 1851.
　　　　　–José de Empáran

translation:

José de Empáran, Political Leader of the County/Region of Veracruz. I certify, that Mr. Julian Workaman [sic] appeared on this day and date, to be listed in the National Guard registry, in compliance with Article 4 of the Constitutional Law, issued on 15 July 1848. Veracruz, 6 February 1851.
　　　　　–José de Empáran

William's granddaughter Josephine was a Hollywood star of the silent era, with 70 Westerns to her credit in the second decade of the twentieth century. David's youngest son, William Henry Workman, was a distinguished Mayor of Los Angeles in 1887 and 1888, before becoming the City Treasurer with responsibility for early financial planning for the 250-mile aqueduct project that brought Owens River water into LA in 1913, setting the stage for the rise of the motion picture industry and the city's most phenomenal growth. Aged 73 in 1912, William Henry enjoyed a fabulous European tour with his wife Maria and daughter Mary Julia, and realized a lifetime's ambition to see the old Workman home at Clifton.

William Henry Workman's older brother Elijah had travelled to Clifton from Los Angeles in 1879, to sell up the remaining Workman property in the village with the assistance of the family's Penrith solicitors, Cant and Fairer. He was followed 25 years later by his nephew, 30-year-old William Henry Jr, son of ex-mayor William Henry, who visited the ancestral home at Clifton and toured the Penrith area in May 1904, during a world cruise that was part of his convalescence after a serious illness.

Writing home to his father, William Henry Jr enthused about Lowther Park with its deer and Ullswater's 'sylvan scenery', and said of Penrith:

> Penrith is a substantial, quaint old town. We got there on market day when the principal streets are filled with farmers' wagons full of produce which they have brought to exchange for the harness and ploughs, shoes and calico, that the shop keepers too have brought out for the barter. The streets are all well macadamized, there are stone pavements all about. The houses look clean and well kept, and the predominance of plate glass windows shows that the people are not poor. All the kids and some of the big people too wear shoes with wooden soles with a bit of brass or copper tacked over the toe. A troupe of them going along the highway make almost as much noise as Japanese in their wooden sandals.

Nothing, it is said, has defined America and the character of its people more than the nation's westward expansion. Certain it is that the Wild West, that most potent symbol of the American dream, was won at terrible cost to those already living there – and to the pioneers who set out to make it theirs. Whatever the story's contradictions, the territorial expansionist who claimed it was America's Manifest Destiny to spread across a vast continent from the Atlantic to the Pacific could have had no better champions for his cause than David and William Workman. Their stories were the stuff that made America.

Anthony Trollope at Penrith
World-famous novelist who invented the Post Office Pillar-box

Anthony Trollope was a prodigious Victorian literary success story, with a 35-year run of 47 novels, 42 short stories, five travel books and many other works to his credit, besides long-term service with the Post Office and worldwide travel. It all started with a lonely life in London and began to take off with a meeting between the two most profound influences on his life as a writer – his wife and his mother. They met at Penrith.

'Carleton Hill' at Penrith was agog that summer of 1844. New owners John and Cecilia Tilley had little time for their view over Brougham Castle and the panorama of the Eden Valley. Cecilia's brother Anthony was coming from Ireland with his new wife Rose, and her mother was on her way from Italy with favourite son Tom.

Anthony Trollope was born in London on 24 April 1815, fifth of seven children of unsuccessful barrister Thomas Anthony Trollope and his vivacious wife Frances. Neglected at home and bullied at Harrow and Winchester schools, Anthony was a troubled 19-year-old when he became a clerk with the Post Office, more by dint of the right family connections than by any particular merit. His job was boring and he was not very good at it, but at least he could daydream at his desk and observe human nature in a way that would be useful to him when he started to write – much like his experiences of getting into debt and bad company at his dismal lodgings in seedy Marylebone.

A colleague of Anthony's at the Post Office near St Paul's was a young man called John

Anthony Trollope (1815-82)

Frances Trollope (1780-1863)

Tilley, who became a close friend of the Trollope family and married Anthony's sister Cecilia Frances in 1839. Tilley had just been promoted to a well-paid Post Office position as Surveyor of the Northern District of England, effectively district manager, and this took him and Cecilia up to Penrith, where they set up home on Fellside below the Beacon and soon started a family.

Anthony and Cecilia's mother was as remarkable for her qualities of resilience and energy as their colourless father was not. As the Trollope family fortunes declined in 1827, the spirited Frances crossed the Atlantic to spend four years in Ohio on a doomed mission to sell European essentials of life to supposedly deprived Americans. Coming back home when the money ran out, she organised the indigent family's 'moonlight flit' to Belgium in 1834 where her hapless husband died soon after.

Frances Trollope had suffered the loss of four children in their infancy and was naturally anxious about Cecilia, her only surviving daughter who was not particularly robust. Throwing herself into writing and soon rewarded with success as a novelist, Frances Trollope was 60 years of age when she visited Penrith in 1840. Having resolved to build a house and make her home in Cumberland to be near her daughter and grandchildren, she bought a four-acre plot of land at Carleton from Sir George Musgrave of Edenhall. This was in January 1841, and Frances and son Tom were able to move into their new home, 'Carleton Hill', eighteen months later.

However, the much-travelled novelist and socialite Frances could not settle at Carleton Hill. She was inclined to blame the Cumbrian weather but seemingly she was not impressed with her northern neighbours either. In any event, she had hardly got the garden planted with trees and shrubs when she sold the Carleton property to her son-in-law John Tilley and his wife Cecilia and decamped with her ever-loyal son Tom for sunny Florence and their welcoming Casa Berti.

Meanwhile, Anthony had been rescued from the doldrums by a Post Office move to Ireland, a posting that would keep him out of England, off and on, for seventeen years (despite a reference from London damning him as 'worthless and unlikely to stay on'). There at last he began to feel at ease with himself.

Anthony was at the seaside resort of Dun Laoghaire near Dublin in July 1842 when he met 22-year-old Rose Heseltine, on holiday there with her bank manager father from Rotherham in Yorkshire. This was just as his mother and brother were moving into Carleton Hill, and over at Penrith a month later his sister Cecilia Tilley found him 'a very different man.'

Anthony Trollope began his first novel, *The Macdermotts of Ballycloran*, soon after he and Rose got engaged. They married in Rotherham (where the local newspaper identified the bridegroom as 'the son of the celebrated authoress, Mrs Trollope') in June 1844, and made plans to visit Penrith together for the first time, immediately after their honeymoon in the Lake District.

Mrs Frances Trollope and son Tom detached themselves from their high-flying Florentine social life among dignitaries like the Grand Duke and Duchess of Modena at the Pitti Palace and British government minister Lord Holland, and arrived back at Carleton Hill to meet the newly-weds – although they did not attend the wedding in Rotherham, for reasons best known to the socially ambitious Mrs Trollope. As it turned out, however, the family get-together at Penrith was a great success. The two Mrs Trollopes, Frances and Rose, got on well, with Rose finding her mother-in-law 'the life and soul of the party.'

Mrs Frances Trollope returned to Italy with Tom, while back in Ireland with his new wife Rose, Anthony pressed on with *The Macdermotts of Ballycloran*. He now had the support and esteem of a strong and dependable woman – and a deadline to meet.

By the summer of 1845 Anthony had finished his first novel and was back at Penrith with Rose, where again they met his mother at Carleton Hill. While Anthony had always felt undervalued as a writer by his family, his influential mother now agreed to place his new manuscript with a minor London publisher, who got *The Macdermotts of Ballycloran* into print to mixed reviews by 1847 – the same year, incidentally, that the Bronte sisters' *Jane Eyre* and *Wuthering Heights* appeared.

Anthony was in the west of England on Post Office business in 1851 when he had his inspired idea for the pillar-box. Despite his burgeoning success as a writer, he stayed on with the Post Office for another sixteen years and died in London in 1882. His beloved wife Rose, who had checked his manuscripts and been his soulmate for 40 years, lived on to the age of 97, and died in 1917.

Several of Anthony Trollope's works show evidence of quite intimate knowledge of the Lake District, particularly the Penrith area. He is best known for his Barchester and Palliser series of novels, and his stories of political and ecclesiastical intrigue have made him essential reading for politicians, peers and clergymen. His fans are said to include former prime ministers Harold Macmillan and John Major, Downton Abbey creator Lord Fellowes, P. D. James and Ruth Rendell. Even non-readers will know that the red pillar-box has long since joined other familiar British icons like the double-decker bus and Nelson's Column.

John Tilley's continuing success with the Post Office was marred by tragedy in his private life. His wife Cecilia, whose health had never been good, died of tuberculosis in 1849, followed within two years by four of their five young children. He soon remarried but his second wife died after just eighteen months. Having married for the third time in 1861, he became Secretary of the Post Office, being made a C.B. ten years later and K.C.B. when he retired in 1880. Sir John Tilley died at his London home aged 85 in 1898.

Henry Bloom Noble
The Isle of Man's greatest benefactor

Westmorland-born Henry Bloom Noble had a major impact on the life of the Isle of Man, as is evident from eponymous institutions there such as Noble's Isle of Man Hospital, Noble's Park and the original Noble's Hospital, which is now the Manx Museum. Less familiar Noble benefactions include St Ninian's church in Douglas and Ramsey Cottage Hospital, while Villa Marina, the great man's residence for 35 years, became the entertainment centre in the heyday of the island's tourist industry, and many educational initiatives owe their existence to him.

Such was Noble's wealth in later life that he could rescue the Isle of Man Steam Packet Company from financial difficulties, make a substantial loan to Douglas Corporation when cash ran short, and even raise the funds to restore confidence in a badly shaken bank.

However the man is a paradox, if not an enigma. His baptismal name was Henry Noble: the Bloom came later. In a remarkable story of 'rags to riches', a poverty-stricken infancy in an English village nurtured a prodigy of Victorian enterprise who flourished on Manx soil. Though pre-eminent in the world of business, Noble lived unostentatiously and did not aspire to high public office. His long life was dedicated to the ruthless pursuit of wealth, yet his huge fortune was left to charity. He never courted popularity, but won his place as the Isle of Man's greatest benefactor.

Henry Bloom Noble was born at the small Westmorland village of Clifton, near Penrith, and baptised plain Henry Noble on 18 June 1816, the elder son of impoverished tenant farmer John Noble and his wife Mary, née Bloom.

John Noble had arrived at Clifton in 1803 with cash in his pocket from a land sale at the family farm a few miles away, but by the time he married Mary at Clifton church in January 1815, 35-year-old John's money and his luck had run out. Unknown to his bride at the time, he had even been arrested in London for debt.

Mary was nearly 40 and had problems of her own. Her late father was an educated Londoner who had run the Earl of Lonsdale's prestigious carpet factory at Lowther for many years but had suffered decades of inescapable penury because he had never been paid his due. Recently widowed and living with her elderly mother and a son from her first marriage, Mary feared she would be left on her own with little money.

So when John Noble and Mary Mason (née Bloom) arrived at the old village church for their nuptials that winter's day in 1815, each thought the other a better prospect than was actually the case. Disillusionment for both of them was not far off when little Henry came on the scene, followed in 1817 by a brother called Thomas.

By early 1818 John and Mary Noble were living apart; he with Henry in miserable lodgings and she with baby Thomas. They were 'as near hungered to death as can be,' as the struggling farmer John put it in a despairing letter to the Earl of Lonsdale of the second creation, who by this time had inherited the title and vast estates of the notorious autocrat who had treated his wife's late father so badly at the carpet factory.

John had read a newspaper report of the death of a customs official at Whitehaven in Cumberland, and he appealed to the Earl to give him the job. Reunited, he and Mary were soon on their way with the children to the busy seaport, where poor little Thomas died aged just two and a half.

Young Henry did well at the highly regarded Piper's Marine School in Whitehaven and got a job with Spittall's, a respected wine and spirit merchants in the town. They also had premises on the Isle of Man, and at the age of nineteen he was on his way over the Irish Sea. He later recalled that he stepped ashore from a schooner on Douglas quayside in 1835 'in clogs and with a single pair of breeches, and they patched.'

It was a good time for an ambitious young man to be landing in Douglas. The Steam Packet Company had started up in 1830, the island's lead mines were booming and tourism was starting, with new buildings going up and the wine and spirits trade profiting as a result. And Henry Bloom Noble – already acknowledging his mother's influence by using her family name – was nothing if not ambitious. Within five years he was managing Spittall's whole Douglas enterprise, and by the age of 25 had set up in opposition to them, as well as launching into property speculation and advertising himself as a money lender.

Later going into shipping, Henry in his early 40s was said to be the richest individual on the island. He was still unmarried and living with his octogenarian mother, who had joined her son in Douglas after the death in

Henry Bloom Noble

Henry Bloom Noble

1850 of her customs official husband in Whitehaven – or perhaps rather before that event – and was clearly a dominant influence on her son's life. At the age of 45, however, Henry married Rebecca Thompson at Braddan near Douglas. She was two years younger than Henry and well-off.

In 1865 Henry and four other influential businessmen founded the Isle of Man Banking Company. In the same year he donated a magnificent stained glass east window – then the finest in the Isle of Man – to St George's church in Douglas. Congregations and visitors to the already impressive church could contemplate the public-spirited generosity – not to say unfailing business instincts – of a benefactor who could proclaim his identity in illuminated script just big enough to be visible to all within the building – PRESENTED BY HENRY BLOOM NOBLE, 1865.

In 1868 he paid £7,750 for the Villa Marina mansion house on Douglas seafront, the former residence of Governor Pigott, and moved in with his wife and mother and their domestic staff. Mary Noble died there the following year, aged 93. Clearly a formidable lady, Mary had seen how badly her parents had been treated at the Lowther carpet factory by the despotic Sir James Lowther, later first Earl of Lonsdale (whose story appears elsewhere in this book), and she must have been determined to see that her son Henry made the most of his talents as a businessman.

In 1886 Henry, perhaps influenced by his philanthropic wife, financed the construction of the original Noble's Hospital in Douglas, the building which now houses the Manx Museum. The foundation stone was laid by Rebecca on 26 July 1886, and she died less than two years later.

Business was never far from Henry Bloom Noble's mind. In 1888 he came to the rescue of the struggling Isle of Man Steam Packet Company with a £20,000 loan. Anticipating a demand for public ownership of the Douglas Waterworks Company, he had acquired a controlling interest in the company and was its chairman when Douglas Town Council set out to buy it in 1890. The waterworks company set a figure of £146,000. After unsuccessful efforts at negotiation, the council's cheque, drawn on Dumbell's Bank, was passed to chairman Henry, who rejected it and demanded – and got – payment in cash!

Dumbell's Bank crashed in 1900, ruining investors and tradesmen and keeping the accountants busy for the next twenty years. Signs of a 'run' on the Isle of Man Banking Company – Noble's bank – were checked when he said he was prepared to back it with all the resources at his disposal. The credit standing of Douglas itself was shaken by the collapse of Dumbell's Bank, and Henry stepped in with a £40,000 loan. It was his last big deal.

Henry Bloom Noble died at his Villa Marina on 2 May 1903. He had come a long way from his poverty-stricken childhood in the village of Clifton in Westmorland, but his birthplace was emblazoned on his granite memorial obelisk in Braddan churchyard.

Henry turned out to be worth over £270,000 – well over £10 million at early 21st century rates. He held the mortgages on 42 properties and had stocks and shares in 42 companies, including the Isle of Man Banking Company, Douglas Gas Light Company, Isle of Man Steam Packet Company, Great Laxey Mining Company, Snaefell Mining Company, Douglas Town Stock and Ramsey Town Stock. He had nearly £10,000 in cash at the bank.

Apart from the Villa Marina, he owned 32 houses between Castletown and Laxey, along with 20 shops, thirteen gardens and 29 plots of land. The large Sefton Hotel in Douglas came into Henry's estate soon after his death when the owners went bankrupt with massive debts in his favour.

Henry's will caused quite a stir. Apart from a few small bequests to his personal staff and relatives on his late wife's side, he left everything to char-

The Henry Bloom Noble memorial obelisk at Braddan. While Clifton was mentioned on a Noble memorial, Henry's younger brother Thomas was forgotten.

ity with £10,000 set aside to build St Ninian's church in Douglas. However, the bulk of the estate was left with trustees under the no-nonsense chairmanship of Henry's old clergyman friend the Very Reverend William Lefroy, Dean of Norwich, who were to distribute the proceeds for charitable purposes as they saw fit.

Funded entirely by the H. B. Noble Trustees, Ramsey Cottage Hospital opened in 1907 and Noble's Park, Douglas, in 1909. The Villa Marina was sold to Douglas Corporation for £60,000 and redeveloped as a major entertainment centre. A new Noble's Hospital in Westmoreland Road, Douglas, was opened in 1912 at an eventual cost of £52,000. Nearly as much went on various educational initiatives, including university scholarships and places at the Island's King William's College, and £33,000 was spent on a children's home in Douglas.

A stockily-built man just 5 feet 6 inches in height, Henry Bloom Noble was a highly intelligent and industrious individual who seized his opportunities to become the most successful Manx businessman of the time, despite – or perhaps because of – his poor start in life across the water in England. While his assiduous pursuit of wealth did not always endear him to his contemporaries, his posthumous reputation was assured by the terms of his will.

However not everyone was happy with Noble's will. Back at Clifton in Westmorland, the eccentric (and reputedly bibulous) rector, the Revd William McClelland Keys-Wells MA, reached for his parish register and the red ink and scrawled across the 1816 record of Henry's baptism: 'This man went to the Isle of Man, died there and left a large sum of money for charitable and other purposes but nothing to the place of his birth!'

Captain John Noble and the *Tayleur*
'White Star' ship went down on its maiden voyage with great loss of life

Managed by the White Star Line, the biggest English merchant ship then afloat went down in 1854 on its maiden voyage with great loss of life. It was not the *Titanic* but the *Tayleur*, and the tragedy happened 58 years before the most famous peacetime sea disaster of all time.

It was a breezy Thursday morning in January when Penrith-born Captain John Noble gave the order to cast off from the Liverpool quayside for the 12,000-mile voyage to Melbourne, Australia. The 656 passengers and crew who faced those turbulent months of shipboard confinement on the Atlantic and Indian Ocean to the far side of the world, would get no further than the other side of the Irish Sea, and 374 of them would perish before the week was out.

Gold fever was in the air in the mid-nineteenth century. California had seen it in 1849; now it was Australia's turn, and people had to get there fast. Victorian business confidence abounded in the afterglow of the Great Exhibition of 1851, and ships were getter bigger. With six ships already trading profitably with America and Australia, the White Star Line ordered a vessel to beat all rivals – the same hope that would eventually produce the ill-fated *Titanic*. The *Tayleur* was launched into the Mersey at Warrington in September 1853 and was towed down to Liverpool for fitting out.

White Star publicity for the *Tayleur* proclaimed: 'This truly splendid vessel, just launched and the largest merchantman yet built in England, will undoubtedly prove to be the fastest of the Australian fleet as she has been constructed expressly with the object of attaining the highest rate of speed. Her vast dimensions enable the owners to provide passenger accommodation not to be met in any vessel afloat . . .'

An iron-hulled ship of 1,997 tons, the nineteenth century's 'Titanic' was named after Charles Tayleur, owner of the world-famous Vulcan engineering works at Warrington and of the Bank Quay foundry where the vessel was built. The 'magnificent new frigate-like ship' was first advertised to sail on 20 October 1853, but that date was optimistic by three months – and

A publicity poster of the time announcing the Tayleur's maiden voyage to Melbourne..

passengers boarding in January found riggers still hard at work.

Captain John Noble had engaged the 65-strong crew (at £2 to £3 a month) in Liverpool in the week before he was due to sail. All except the third mate were strangers to him, and many were foreigners – including Chinese, Lascars and Nubians – with little or no grasp of English. Even more ominously, there would be no sea trial.

The *Tayleur* finally left Liverpool at 11.55am on Thursday, 19 January 1854 and headed out into the Irish Sea under the command of a pilot, who left her in darkness off Holyhead at about 7.30pm. Soon after, the south-easterly wind began to increase into a gale; but the motley crew who had given the ship a full spread of canvas when conditions were good were not inclined to go aloft and shorten sail when things got rough. Frightened passengers who ventured up on deck in the early hours of Friday found sails torn and flapping wildly in the howling wind.

The new leviathan was proving very hard to handle. With the wind from the south-east, she had sailed well enough along the North Wales coast, but in layman's terms she would not turn left off Anglesey, to head south. The new ropes were very stiff and she was slow in responding to the rudder. But that was not all. Visibility was poor, and the iron-hulled ship's three compasses all showed different readings. Captain Noble did not know where he was, and the dreadful truth was that he was not heading south at all but west towards Ireland.

As dawn broke on Saturday morning the lookout spotted 'land ahead.' It was Lambay Island, just off the Irish coast near Dublin. Soon the terrified passengers could see the waves breaking on the rocky shore of the island, but the ship was now completely out of control and at the mercy of the wind. In a last desperate effort to avert disaster, Captain Noble ordered both anchors let go, but the cables parted. Nothing could save the drifting ship and she was swept broadside on to rocks just off the island with fearful violence.

Panic broke out on deck as the great ship was pounded against the rocks and started sinking by the stern. Every wave carried off scores of struggling people until only the masts showed above the water. It was noon on Saturday, 21 January, and the *Tayleur's* ambitious maiden voyage had ended after just 48 hours.

Just two miles offshore, Lambay Island was uninhabited apart from an occasional coastguard. Rescuers who battled against the storm to get to the island by steamer from Dublin more than 24 hours later found a terrible

The site of the sinking of the Tayleur in the Irish Sea

scene. The shoreline near the wreck was strewn with flotsam and dead bodies – hundreds of them. The ghastly sight was made even worse by scavengers picking over the corpses.

Survivors of the sinking – and of subsequent exposure to the atrocious weather on Lambay Island – numbered just 282, and many of them were badly injured. It was an awful irony that most of the ship's passengers were Irish emigrants who had just left their famine-wracked homeland in hope of a better future far away.

Captain Noble had stayed with his ship to the last and then managed to save himself. The inquest at nearby Malahide found he had acted with coolness and courage in the final emergency, although he was criticised for continuing the voyage after he discovered the compass problem. The primary blame for the 'deplorable accident' was laid at the door of the owners for sending the vessel to sea with faulty compasses and without a sea trial.

John Noble was born in Great Dockray, Penrith, where his father was in business as a butcher, and he was baptised at the town's St Andrew's church on 29 May 1825. His father died suddenly nine years later and young John was sent to the busy seaport of Whitehaven to live with an uncle who was a customs official.

John went to sea as a young man and married the daughter of a Whitehaven publican. He did well at his job – and he had the right family connections in the shipping business, which would have helped – and was just 28 years of age when the White Star Line gave him command of their much-heralded new sailing ship, the *Tayleur,* then under construction at Warrington in Lancashire.

Though he survived the disaster that cost so many lives, poor Captain John Noble never really recovered from the emotional after-effects. He took to drink and did not get the support he expected from his wife, who eventually left him in failing health at their home in Great George Street, Liverpool, and went off to London with a commercial traveller. John died at the age of 36 on 24 July 1861 and went to his last resting place in Smithdown Road cemetery, Liverpool. He left no family.

James Barker Bland
Footloose farmer with intellectual interests

Blands have long been well known Lakeland farmers, not to mention wrestlers and fell-runners as well as the odd sculptor and writer. Although a son of the land, James Barker Bland was in a class of his own. Born at Hegdale near Shap in the old county of Westmorland on 22 August 1854, thirteenth of the fourteen children of John and Elizabeth Bland, JBB (as he became known) was described by the *Whitehaven News* in 1942 as 'a truly remarkable man who was one of Cumberland's best known characters.'

Sheep farmer John Bland and his wife Elizabeth moved house a few times in the 23 years they were together before James Barker came on the scene. Leaving home at Kentmere with their first-born around 1834, they trekked over the fells to the Eden Valley, where four more offspring joined them. Then they moved back west to 'Flakehow' in Mardale – destined to disappear under Haweswater reservoir – where they lived for a decade or so while enlarging the family by another half-dozen. After JBB at Hegdale in 1854, they had their fourteenth and last at Shap and were back over the hills at Kentmere Hall by 1861.

JBB left home at Kentmere for Patterdale when he was just sixteen, later claiming he made that rough ten-mile hike over Garburn and Kirkstone passes 25 times before finally settling at the foot of Kirkstone. He was working at Caudalebeck Farm near Brotherswater when he met 23-year-old local farmer's daughter Esther Thompson, and they were married at the valley's St Patrick's Church on 4 January 1876. He and Esther moved into Sykeside cottage and four of their seven children were born there before their big move of the 1880s.

It was a wintry morning early in 1883 when JBB and a less enthusiastic Esther got the children out of bed and packed their belongings for a 20-mile trek over precipitous Kirkstone, Wrynose and Hardknott passes – at one go in two carts, they say – to the ancient Brotherilkeld sheep farm in Eskdale, where JBB soon had a workforce of three, as well as his seven children.

James Barker Bland

High outgoings (or maybe it was tight-fistedness) may explain why he once wanted two children baptised at the same time and told the surprised parson at St Catherine's church down the valley, 'Well, it wasn't worth yocking up t' cart for just yan o' them.'

A tall strong man, if perhaps a bit lame because of a childhood ligament injury, JBB walked an awful lot. One day, the story goes, he set off on foot from Brotherilkeld over Hardknott and Wrynose for Kendal market by way of the Windermere steamer and then the train for the last few miles. As it turned out, he got to Ambleside at the head of the lake just in time to see the boat leaving Waterhead pier, so he just turned round and walked back home again. In the 1890s, though, he took the whole family back east from Eskdale over those two rough mountain passes – and Kirkstone as well,

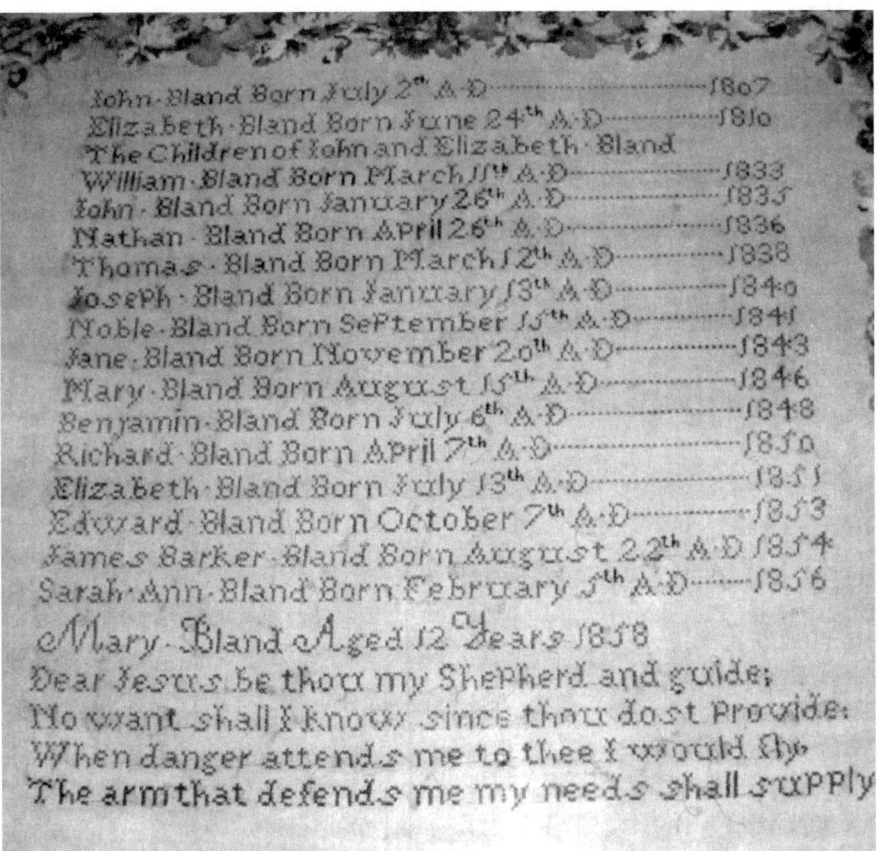

A Bland family sampler of 1858, made by twelve year old Mary Bland.

passing Sykeside in Patterdale where they started their marital adventure twenty years before – all the way to Waterside Farm at the east end of Ullswater near Pooley Bridge.

JBB soon had to tell his wife that the family were off west again. By 1897 the Blands were living in lonely Ennerdale, although not for long – a dispute between JBB and the land agent over fencing may have had something to do with it. This restless family were soon at Scar Green near Calderbridge, until JBB took the tenancy of nearby Laverock How, which he was to call home for most of the rest of his life. JBB passed away at his eldest son John's farm on the Corney fellside near Bootle on 10 January 1942 and was laid to rest in Ponsonby churchyard alongside Esther from Patterdale, who had been his ever-dutiful wife for 57 years when she died in 1933.

JBB was surely footloose: even in his 70s he would walk the twenty miles over the Cold Fell track from Calderbridge to Cockermouth on market day. He was his own man and didn't always see eye to eye with his landlords. But it was much more than his individuality and itchy feet that made him such a hit with the *Whitehaven News*, for he was an authoritative contributor to the respected West Cumberland newspaper on local archaeology, history and folklore, as well as on farming topics. His grasp of historical facts and dates was legendary, as was his knowledge of writers like Macaulay, Boswell and Byron. He could recite from memory long passages from Rabbie Burns and was a popular visitor to Burns Night gatherings as far afield as Moffat – over the Border in Scotland but you could get there by train in those days.

JBB was also in demand as a raconteur with a keen sense of humour. One of his tales concerned the cynical countryman who was asked about his plans for his two sons.

'Well,' JBB recalled him saying, 'T' older lad's a likely chap an' gey smart. Aa think Aa'll mek a mowdy catcher of him; but t'other's nobbut a maudlin an' fit to be nowt but a parson.'

Then there was the farmer in 'middlin' fettle' who went to see a doctor and was advised to give up smoking and drinking. The ailing farmer muttered his thanks and made to leave when the doctor asked for his fee.

'Fee? What's ta wantin' a fee for?' asked the farmer. 'For my professional advice of course,' said the medic.

'Thoo'll git neea fee frae me, cos Aa's nut tekkin' thee advice!' came the retort.

James Barker Bland

James Barker Bland and family, photographed in 1926.

False modesty was not one of JBB's weaknesses. Did Beatrix Potter really have him in mind with her *Tale of Pigling Bland?*

'That piglet is a right ratch, just like you, Bland,' the great lady is supposed to have said of the runt of a litter of hers that had a habit of wandering away from home. Or was he just out to impress with a tall tale? Whatever, this formidable pair of Lakeland sheep breeders must have met, if not socially then perhaps at one of the local agricultural shows they were both fond of.

Life-long sheep farmer James Barker Bland was equally at home with his varied intellectual pursuits as he was with his animals, a self-taught polymath and bibliophile if not something of an enigma. Elderly descendants who remembered him as 'a right grumpy old beggar' were quick to say he was always generous to anyone who sought his advice, especially on legal problems. Perhaps we should leave the last word about him to an old schoolmaster of his who also knew him in later life. The teacher said JBB was a man of immense knowledge of the law who would have been better suited to the legal profession than to farming.

William John Woodhouse
Railwayman's son who became a professor of Greek in Australia

Sydney University's new Professor of Greek was an ambitious and committed classicist who took up his post in 1901. He had come a long way from home in England and would win world renown in Australia.

William John Woodhouse was born on 7 November 1866 at Clifton and Lowther railway station on the Lancaster to Carlisle main line in Westmorland, the eldest son of 26-year-old station master Richard Woodhouse and his ex-schoolteacher wife Mary, née Titterington, from Witherslack near Kendal.

Rail company postings soon took the family away from Clifton to Whitehaven (Bransty) and then on to Sedbergh on the Ingleton branch line, where young William enrolled as a day pupil at Sedbergh School and came under the influence of people like H. W. Fowler, a noted authority on the English language.

William's forté, however, was the classical languages of Latin and Greek. This earned him a scholarship to Queen's College, Oxford, and a BA degree with first class honours in Classics, before going on to the British School of Archaeology in Athens and specialising in excavations at the ancient site of Megalopolis. He took his Oxford MA degree and won the coveted Conington Prize, and two years' topographical exploration of little known Aetolia in Greece led to publication of a substantial book.

In 1897 he was appointed lecturer in Classics at the University College of North Wales in Bangor. He also found time to marry Eleanor Emma Jackson at Sedbergh Church, while preparing school editions of Greek and Latin authors and contributing to several other works of scholarship.

Three years later he secured a lecturer's position at the leading Scottish university of St Andrews but had been there little over a year when he and Eleanor, with three-year-old son Richard and baby Liska, left the UK for a prestigious appointment on the far side of the world.

Woodhouse was 34 when he became professor of Greek at the University of Sydney, a position he was to hold for the next 36 years. His other

William John Woodhouse

Sedbergh Station, photographed in about 1900.

university appointments at Sydney would include serving as curator of the Nicholson Museum, dean of the Faculty of Arts and fellowship of the Senate, while for many years he was also a member of the local bursary endowment board and a trustee of the Library of New South Wales.

Throwing himself energetically into his new life on the other side of the world, Professor Woodhouse took personal responsibility for the whole Greek course at Sydney University, while sometimes also filling in for Latin. As a teacher, he was regarded as rather unorthodox but highly effective, his scholarly and engaging lectures often seasoned with liberal anecdotes and a mischievous sense of humour. A painstaking researcher and a stickler for punctuality as well as a humorist, it was said he would sometimes arrive before his students and start a lecture without them!

With his wife Eleanor and their two children, he set up home initially in the remote Blue Mountains, living during the week in Sydney boarding houses. Later on he moved to an outer suburb that involved tedious train journeys on which he occupied himself by studying Albanian, Bulgarian and Hebrew.

Despite the distance, Woodhouse revisited his beloved Greece three times: in 1908 when he collected a sculpture for the Nicholson Museum, in 1921 when returning from an international university congress in Oxford, and finally in 1935. He withdrew somewhat from university affairs in later years to garner the fruit of his scholarship in three books which established his international reputation: *The composition of Homer's Odyssey* (Oxford 1930, reprinted 1969), *King Agis of Sparta and his campaign in Arcadia in 418BC* (Oxford 1931, reprinted 1977) and *Solon the Liberator* (published posthumously in 1938 and reprinted in 1965).

Professor Woodhouse's health failed early in 1937 and he died on 26 October that year at his home in Nelson Street, Gordon, Sydney. He was survived by his wife and their two children. A memorial fund was used to buy Greek vases for the Nicholson Museum.

William John Woodhouse was succeeded by a man of formidable intellect, a Cambridge graduate who aimed to be the foremost classical scholar of his generation and wanted to be a professor at a younger age than the German philosopher Nietzsche, who had achieved that status at the age of 24. Failing in that ambition by a year, John Enoch Powell was still just 25 when he was awarded the chair of Greek at Sydney University – the youngest professor in the British Empire – and he might have stayed in academia but for the war.

An improbable soldier, Powell returned to England to enlist as a private in the Royal Warwicks when war broke out in September 1939, and was recruited from the kitchens for intelligence service training after addressing a senior officer in classical Greek. He finished the war as the British Army's youngest brigadier, aged 32, despite never coming nearer action than hearing the advancing German guns while at 8th Army GHQ.

Joseph Scott – 'Mr Los Angeles'

Penrith-born emigrant to fame and fortune in California, USA

Abraham Lincoln's gaunt features in bronze accompany his Gettysburg Address in front of Los Angeles County Court. Nearby stands the statue of a man in a suit on a pedestal with the inscription:

'JOSEPH SCOTT, 'MR LOS ANGELES', 1867-1958,
Beloved citizen, distinguished lawyer, civic leader
Practiced law in Los Angeles from 1894 to 1958
Established Knights of Columbus in California 1902
Served as President of the Chamber of Commerce, Board of Education
Community Chest, Boys' Week and Draft Board
Stalwart champion of Americanism and militant foe of communism
Lifelong crusader for recognition of the Irish Republic
Nominated Herbert Hoover for President of the United States
Recognized by Church and State with highest honors many times.'

The Scott statue was erected on Grand Avenue in Los Angeles in the early 1960s. A decade earlier, a fulsome tribute to Joseph Scott by Californian Congressman Gordon McDonough in the United States House of Representatives had opened with these lofty sentiments:

'A youthful Scottish-Irish immigrant to the United States who moved among and was the equal of the giants of his day in all walks of life, but who never lost the common touch of the ordinary man. A great humanitarian, defender of the weak, protector of the poor, a master in the courts, an unequaled expounder of the law of the land in pursuit of justice, scornful of the powerful who would oppress the weak. Champion of the dignity of man in the image and likeness of God. Defender of his faith, Christian gentleman, as humble as sackcloth and ashes, as majestic as a king, statesman, scholar, poet, a good father and husband, a friend of humanity.

'Joseph Scott grew up with Los Angeles from the time it was a sleepy pueblo to its present metropolitan status as the third largest city in the United States. In spite of his 85 years, he is still active every day in his law practice and in court. This is not only a story of the life of Joe Scott. It is also a historical account of Los Angeles and of the many outstanding events in the Nation in which he participated.'

In his 65 years in Los Angeles Scott saw the city's population of 60,000 in the 1890s mushroom to millions in the twentieth century as the Owens River aqueduct brought water from the Sierra Nevada Mountains and Hollywood made it the world's entertainment capital, while he made a giant contribution to its development in many fields. With his formidably bushy eyebrows and shock of white hair, he was a charismatic figure and a spellbinding orator who won fame as a tireless opponent of racial and religious intolerance. As a lawyer, his combativeness inside the courtroom was as legendary as his charity outside.

Joseph Scott was born at the market town of Penrith in the old English county of Cumberland on 17 July 1867, second of eight sons of a Scots-Presbyterian father and an Irish Catholic mother. Cockermouth-born Joseph Scott, senior, was a 26-year-old Penrith newspaper printer when he married Mary Donnelly in Wexford in 1862, despite her family's misgivings on religious grounds (but with the blessing of the wise old priest who married them), and their son William Isaac was born in Ireland in 1863, before they left for England. Joseph junior had great respect for his father, who never objected to his nine children being raised as Catholics, but he always insisted, 'I am what I am by reason of my mother.'

Poor and barely literate, Mary Donnelly from tiny Duncormick had lived at Enniscorthy in the shadow of Vinegar Hill, where British guns killed 500 Wexford pikemen in the Irish uprising of 1798, and had seen shell-shocked Irishmen coming home from Gettysburg. Her son Joseph was born during a frightening Cumbrian thunderstorm, and Joseph senior recalled Mary's whispered prophecy about their newborn son – 'He came to me in thunder and lightning. He'll ride the hurricane all his life.'

Just three months later Mary was outraged by the hanging in industrial Manchester of three young Irish Fenians for shooting a policeman. Such was her distress at what happened to 'these mere boys... no more felons than any American Revolutionary hero... they wanted to make Ireland free...' that she would tell young Joseph she had knelt over his crib and said, 'I prayed for them and my tears fell upon your face, and you were baptised a second time.' Deeply moved, Joseph would always see this 'second baptism' as the gift of a love for, and a pledge to, freedom.

Many years later, a Los Angeles dinner marking Joseph Scott's 50 years

Joseph Scott's statue in Los Angeles.

in America was attended by the great and good of California, among them a US ambassador to the Irish Republic, a federal judge, an archbishop and former president of the United States Herbert Hoover. When a speaker remarked on Scott's conspicuous religious faith, the great man could still hear his devout Catholic mother murmuring to him, a small boy, as they stood by the crib in the little church near their English home over 60 years before, 'There, my boy, is the helpless Babe, shivering in the manger. In 30 years' time He will be agonizing on the cross. This is the ideal you must follow, boy; that is what you must understand. Always be true to the Star of Bethlehem and Calvary.'

On leaving Ireland, the Scott family lived briefly in Barnsley, Yorkshire, before moving to Penrith. Soon after Joseph's birth in 1867, they went on to Stafford and then up to Darlington in County Durham, where Joseph's deep religious faith was nurtured at Ushaw College near Durham city, the Roman Catholic seminary he attended with distinction from 1880 to 1889. While he was most successful in grammar and rhetoric, his best-remembered instructor was an Anglo-Spanish teacher of French – Merry del Val – who became Cardinal Secretary of State to Pope Pius X.

Joseph matriculated at London University but did not not pursue the academic or clerical life that might have been expected of him, explaining years later that there was no place at all for a man of his blood and faith in England in those days. Going on to account for his decision to cross the Atlantic, he said his first conception of America with its ideals of liberty and democracy came from his Irish mother who had told him as a little boy about the Irishmen who came back to county Wexford from America with stories of the gaunt, haggard man who stood at Gettysburg and prayed that 'government of the people, by the people and for the people shall not perish from this earth.'

Joseph's distraught mother and father were at the Liverpool dock to see him off on his great adventure in 1889, and he thought he would never see them again. Joseph and Mary had already had their heartbreaks. Their sixth son, Walter Francis, was just nine months old when he died in 1880 and they had lost eldest son William Isaac at the age of 19 in 1882. They were not to know that fateful day in Liverpool that their youngest son William, then four years old, would die just three years later in 1892, and three more of their eight sons would not live beyond their thirties. Apart from Joseph, the only one of the eight Scott brothers to survive to middle age would be fifth son Frederick, who was destined to follow his brother Joseph to California and live out his retirement in San Diego.

Joseph had barely parted from his parents when he was held on the ship's gangplank and briefly detained as an Army deserter in a case of mistaken identity, but he arrived in Boston with $50 in his pocket and a letter of introduction to an Irish-American newspaper editor, with hopes of becoming a journalist. Frustrated in that ambition, he shovelled coal in a Massachusetts paper mill for 12 cents an hour and was down to his last two dollars when he got a job as a labourer at 20 cents an hour on a New York building site. 'God forgive me,' he would recall years later at a speaking engagement in Los Angeles, 'it was a Protestant church!'

After just five months in the United States and still only 22 years of age, Joseph's innate Irish eloquence – together with his astute acquisition of an appropriate text-book and some useful insider information from an old friend from Ushaw days – elevated him to professor of rhetoric and English grammar at St Bonaventure's College, Allegheny, New York, where forceful use of his hod-carrier's physique in an early confrontation with a rebellious student established his reputation as a man who was not to be trifled with. At $300 a year, the salary was adequate for Joseph's immediate needs but hardly enough for a man who wanted to marry and raise a family.

In June 1893 he and an equally ambitious friend, Father Joe Noonan, left New York by transcontinental train for California. Robbed of cash and train tickets in a crowded hotel lobby in mid-West Chicago, which was teeming with visitors to the World Fair, they bumped into the world heavyweight boxing champion 'Gentleman Jim' Corbett, soon after his defeat of John L. Sullivan. Corbett, who had known Noonan before he became a priest, was delighted that his old friend Joe was now wearing the collar. Living up to his name, the genial boxer saw the badly shaken travellers' plight and promptly rescued them with a gift of $500.

At the end of that 3,000-mile train trip from the ceaseless bustle of New York, the then small city of Los Angeles made a profound impression on Scott, with its leisurely pace of life in the sun on the plain between the San Gabriel Mountains and the Pacific Ocean. The surrounding countryside, with its citrus and olive groves, dusty desert roads and dilapidated mission churches from the Spanish/Mexican era, put him in mind of the Holy Land.

Scott was introduced by Los Angeles priest Joseph Doyle, a friend from Allegheny who had persuaded him to come out West, to the influential Isidore Dockweiler, head of a leading pioneer family, who rekindled in the young man an interest in the law that had begun in his spare time at Allegheny. Dockweiler had trained as a lawyer himself under Los Angeles judge James Anderson, a Memphis-born former officer in the Confederate Army who, like many others, had come out west to start over again after being impoverished by the Civil War. He suggested going into Anderson's office or that of Judge Stephen White. As White was 'deep in politics', Joseph chose the former option and was soon immersed in his legal studies. That decision won Joseph Scott a long and distinguished – not to say fearless and sometimes controversial – legal career, besides elevating him to the highest echelons of Californian society and enabling him to undertake worldwide travel.

Joseph's boyhood dreams of the Wild West had already been indulged in the United States with a visit to the Iroquois Indians on the Allegheny River. His fascination with the original people of America soon combined with a desire for a break from the law books to take him on a much more dangerous mission, when he supplemented his own Winchester rifle with a pair of borrowed six-guns to join a cowboy posse led by Judge Anderson's son, who happened to be sheriff of Yavapai County, Arizona. Their quarry was the dreaded Apache Kid, a murderous young renegade from an Indian reservation whose three victims in the previous week included the deputy marshal of Phoenix. A gun battle among the cactus left two Indians dead but the wily Kid escaped to fight another day.

Back in Los Angeles, Scott was admitted to the California Bar in 1894 and joined the choir of the city's St Vibiana's Cathedral, where he met, and later married, 27-year-old Bertha Roth from an old San Francisco family with French and Mexican roots. He and Bertha eventually had eleven children, seven of whom survived to adulthood.

'Water is king' was the first phrase that caught Joseph's ear when he was new to Los Angeles. Then not much over a hundred years old and just forty years since it was a sleepy little Mexican pueblo, the place that promised so much was founded on a semi-desert and drought ruined many a dry farmer. The crops, the cattle and all the wealth of the area cried out for water. Men were said to have killed each other for water holes, and the fields dried up for want of the precious liquid. When Joseph was a rookie lawyer in the 1890s, water disputes were everywhere and the courts were jammed with water litigation cases.

Apart from the wells, the young city's main water supply in those days was a small stream that flowed past a place where later a monument stood to the Irishman whose modest home was at that spot and whose job it was to look after the miserable water supply. 'You can't make a city out of that trickle of water,' was visionary Bill Mulholland's contemptuous refrain as he sat looking at the snows on the tops of far-off mountains, dreaming of the day when an aqueduct like ancient Rome's would bring plenty of melted snow for storage and use in the growing but desperately parched community.

A few years later, when Joseph Scott was president of Los Angeles Chamber of Commerce, he appointed a committee of three to survey the aqueduct project to bring water from the Sierra Nevada Mountains. It was going to cost over $25,000,000, right up against the city's bonding limit, but the Chamber approved the proposal by eight to one and the city would soon be on its way to becoming the great metropolis of the West.

Electricity in its early days also threw up an interesting challenge for

Joseph. Newly qualified in 1894, he got out the horse and buggy and braved the dust and sand in his face on the pioneer-like 100-mile drive over desert trails to Palm Springs, to see clients who had a legal problem that gave rise to the question of how far electricity could be transmitted over power lines. As luck would have it, Joseph had recently met and entertained in Los Angeles the wife and daughter of an assistant to the electrical engineer Thomas Edison, and the two ladies had invited him out east to stay with them and meet Edison. Joseph's well-off Palm Springs clients paid his fare for the 6,000-mile return rail trip to New Jersey, and Joseph returned with the great inventor's expert opinion in writing.

Distance was no object to the irrepressible Joseph Scott, as many of his exploits in the early years of the twentieth century would confirm – and so much the better if the journey would allow him to publicise his beloved California. As he said in later life, 'Los Angeles became and remained through the years my number one client without fee. It was very catching.' Needless to say, he was not shy of the limelight himself.

In 1902 Joseph was sent by the Knights of Columbus as a delegate to its national convention in New Haven, on the other side of the United States in Connecticut. Still in his thirties, he was a new member and unknown to that nationwide Catholic organisation until Missouri floods in Kansas marooned his train for three days. As soon as he could, he wired ahead to the convention people and let them know he was going to be very late but that he should be there for the closing dinner. As it turned out, the story of his dramatic escape from the floods really raised his profile with the Knights of Columbus and put him on the list of speakers at the great event – his big moment he thought, albeit as thirteenth out of fourteen speakers.

At the big dinner he was seated next to a boring individual who told him he knew all about California with its biggest oranges, pumpkins and mountains but that he was now on the Atlantic seaboard, the home of Yale: New Haven was the place to be. After-dinner speakers started to take up the theme of boasting about their native States. 'I'm from Massachusetts, the grand old Bay State with its Plymouth Rock... dawn of liberty... Bunker Hill...' Then it was 'What's Massachusetts? Come to Pennsylvania and I'll show you the cradle of liberty... Declaration of Independence... where the Constitution was written...' The New Yorker told of his rich state and the 'city with its banks... the Nation's finances...' The Virginian boasted of George Washington and Jefferson, Monroe and Madison. Then it was the turn of Ohio, the 'state that gave the nation its Presidents,' and so on.

Joseph Scott in his Los Angeles office.

By the time the thirteenth speaker Scott rose to his feet it was well after midnight and the wine bottles were empty. In no mood for any more of the blarney, he announced: 'I'm from California. No doubt you have heard a lot about it. I'll add only this. If Columbus had landed on the Pacific coast, you suckers would still be undiscovered to this day!'

That brief but explosive speech in New Haven would help to bring the next and biggest Knights of Columbus convention to Los Angeles, more than 5,000 delegates in all, and Joseph Scott would be its chairman. More than that, the resulting publicity soon took him on to city bodies like the Board of Education and the Board of the Southwest Museum.

Los Angeles, California, then by train to New Haven, Connecticut; that 3,000-mile marathon with a three-day delay in the middle would surely have been enough for any mere mortal, even if he only had himself to think about. But that is not the whole story, not even half of it in fact.

It all began in Los Angeles with an argument between Joseph and his wife Bertha. Joseph was proud of his first-born son Joe, who was three and a half years old, so proud that he desperately wanted his mother Mary to see the little fellow. He pleaded with Bertha to let him take Joe with him to New Haven and thence to England, and she finally agreed.

In New Haven little Joe got chickenpox and a doctor advised against taking him across the Atlantic, but the child said he felt fine and no spots showed on his face so he was duly bundled up the ship's gangplank. On deck was a lovely little girl of about his own age. His father told him not to speak to her or go near her, and he promised he would not. Two days out at sea, Joseph saw him with the little girl – kissing her full on the face. Soon after, her gentlemanly father came up to Joseph and said, 'Mr Scott, please don't let our little girl near your Joe – she has just broken out with the chickenpox...'

Still, father and son got to England and Mary duly met her little American grandson. Anyone who doubts that outcome should know that a photograph was taken of 35-year-old Joseph flanked by his elderly mother and the little boy. Well preserved, this remarkable picture of a three-generation family group from a third of the way round the world appeared with an article about Joseph Scott in a Los Angeles newspaper 50 years later. Sadly, little Joe's story would not have a happy ending: his doting parents were grief-stricken when they lost him in 1910.

The court cases that would seal Scott's reputation as a hard-hitting advocate soon began to make the headlines, but travel was always in his blood. Defying that 6,000-plus-mile marathon each way by land and by sea, he returned to England to visit his ageing parents in Darlington, County Durham, more than once – indeed as often as his growing family and law practice would allow, as he put it. He must surely have seen his mother again in 1908, although his father Joseph had died the year before.

Joseph was back at Ushaw, Durham, 20 miles from Darlington, as a guest speaker at his old college's 100th anniversary celebrations. When he took his place in the college hall that momentous day in 1908, as an American visitor nervously awaiting his turn to address a large assembly of cardinals, educators and leading public figures of Britain and Europe while wishing he was back in his little Los Angeles office, he was seated next to Canon Rooney, the elderly Irish pastor from his young days in Darlington – and a man who had done much to get him into Ushaw as a boy. Motioning anxiously to the distinguished audience, he turned to his old mentor and said, 'Canon Rooney, I have cold feet.'

Colourful Characters of Cumbria's Eden Valley

```
OFFICE PHONE  HOME A8271              LAW OFFICES OF                    CABLE ADDRESS
         SUNSET MAIN 6880            JOSEPH SCOTT                          "SCOTT"
RESIDENCE PHONE  E 1343
              WEST 1662    706-707-708 EQUITABLE SAVINGS BANK BUILDING
                                      LOS ANGELES, CAL.
```

Oct. 8, 1909.

Reg. Joseph Broadhead,
    Ushaw College,
        Durham, England.

My dear Friend:

    Enclosed find copy of letter received by me from Bishop Conaty written at Ushaw. It is such a charming compliment to the old place that I thought you might like to have his candid sentiments written so confidentially to me as he might not have expressed himself quite so emphaticcaly to your face owing to your native modesty.

    I shall be delighted to hear from you what impression he created among you, particularly as to his address to the students.

    We are now preparing to receive President Taft in Los Angeles and I have to undergo the ordeal, as well as submit the President to the annoyance of hearing my lusty lungs with an east-wind snap exercise themselves for his benefit for a half hour or so. Michael Rushe will probably send you a copy of the papers, as he undertakes to consider himself my staff correspondent.

    Bishop Conaty will return within the next few days as he is hurrying forward to be at home for President Taft's visit.

    With kindest regards to all old friends, believe me, as ever

                   Sincerely yours,

                     Joseph Scott

Enc.

A letter from Joseph Scott to Ushaw College. The letter refers to Scott's preparations for the forthcoming visit to Los Angeles by US President Taft.

Joseph Scott – Mr Los Angeles

1/97/37-4

C O P Y.

Ushaw College, Durham. Sep 19, 09

My dear Joe:

By this you will see that I have tried to keep my word and I am a guest of Ushaw under whose hospitable roof I have spent the Sunday. Fr. Bernard and I left London at ten yesterday and after a pleasant and delightful trip reached Durham at 3. 25 P. M. We soon found ourselves speeding away in a carriage to Ushaw, up hill and down dale as you well know by the Pot and Glass Inn, by the Dog and Gun Inn, until at last we caught a glimpse of St. Cuthberts, hidden among the foliage, in a bower of tree and shrub, an ideal spot for a great College. We came as the boys were returning from their holidays and passed wagon loads of trunks which told of students making their way back to books and exercises. We received a most cordial welcome from the President and Faculty, who all anxiously inquired for you and who were pleased to hear that you kept the white banner flying. Mr. Broadhead was particularly anxious to hear about you and I gave him as fair an account as my tender conscience would permit. I soon visited the Chapels and the building generally and soon realized that you have every reason to be proud of Ushaw, its history, its school and its men. The school term began last evening and every one was present to answer for himself. Nearly three hundred students, ecclesiastical and lay are in attendance and they appear to be a lot of splendid fellows. Today we have High Mass and Vespers and the singing is remarkably good. I have been delighted with it and listened to it from the place of vantage in the gallery. At noon I had the honor of addressing the Faculty and students in the Exhibition, where I am told you carried off the honors at the Centenary and I tried real hard to hold our character as you had made it. I spoke as an old College boy to young men and reminded them of the service expected from Catholic college men, lay as well as clerical. I gave them a little bit of an old boy's experience in the world of affairs and urged them to prepare for the work which they will be called to do. It was a splendid opportunity to emphasize some lessons to three hundred picked youths, and I tried to utilize it. I spent a good part of the afternoon with Mr. Bonney in the Library which has so many treasures, telling of the days when it cost to profess our faith and also giving us a chance to see the rare works which connect us with a glorious past. It is indeed a wonderful library with its 40,000 volumes, and its rich and rare manuscripts. I wish I had time to spend some days here but we must go tomorrow as we sail for home on Saturday. The boys go on retreat tonight. Father Benson is to preach it. I met him here for the first time, a most charming man. The weather is perfect and I leave you to draw upon your memory for a picture of the scenes which present themselves on every side. I am glad for my own sake that I made the journey and I shall never forget what it has meant to me. I thank you for suggesting and urging it.

Yours sincerely,
Hishop.

Copy letter referred to in Joseph Scott's letter dated 8 October 1909..

The serious-minded old priest looked at him with concern and replied, 'Joseph, that's serious. You must not neglect yourself. Cold feet is a sign of incipient pneumonia.' Joseph had not intended to mislead the kindly priest with unfamiliar American slang, but at least the humour of the situation calmed his nerves – and the audience was good to him, as was the English press who commented on his address. In any event, he saw that 1908 invitation to Ushaw as the greatest honour of his life up to that time, and it would remain with him as one of his fondest memories.

In a sensational case of 1911, Scott took on the defence of the two McNamara brothers, union men accused of dynamiting the *Los Angeles Times* building in furtherance of a dispute with the bitterly anti-union owner, General Harrison Gray Otis, a tough and uncompromising veteran of the Civil War and the 1898 Spanish-American war in the Philippines – and hitherto an admirer of Scott as an 'Irish' immigrant who shared the publisher's Republican politics. The outcome went way beyond what the reckless conspirators had intended, for a gas main was breached in the explosion and 22 workers were killed. It was Scott's view that the two defendants would only avoid the death penalty if they pleaded guilty, and they were eventually persuaded to do so with the assistance of the prison chaplain. This had the desired effect, and one of the McNamara brothers got life imprisonment while the other was sentenced to fifteen years.

Always the missionary zealot as well as the wily lawyer, Joseph Scott was said to have spent even more time trying to bring the wayward McNamara brothers back to their Catholic faith than representing them in court. However, that 1911 criminal trial ended the friendship between Scott and Otis, and damaging allegations were published repeatedly in the *Los Angeles Times* over the next four years as Otis attacked Scott in print and also in cartoons often portraying him as a hod-carrier, then a common caricature of the mostly working-class Irish immigrants.

Matters came to a head early in 1915, when the *Los Angeles Times* claimed that Scott had grossly mishandled a divorce case by persuading a wealthy lady client to file for divorce, against her true wishes. Brushing aside the fears of concerned friends who urged caution in dealing with the hitherto all-powerful newspaper, Joseph started an action for libel which finally went in his favour. Awarded unprecedented damages of $47,700, he displayed a photograph of the cheque on the wall of his office. He always saw this bitter clash with the *Los Angeles Times* as a crisis, the turning point of his life.

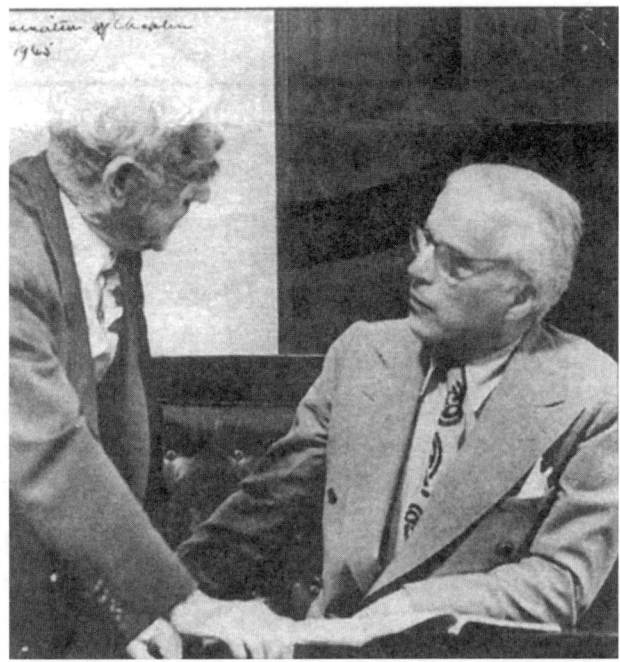

Joseph Scott, left, cross-examines Charlie Chaplin in a 1945 paternity suit.

Now turned 50 and a man of some wealth, Joseph moved his family out to Pasadena's Orange Grove Boulevard, the city's so-called millionaires' row along the Arroyo Seco. Otis died that same year, 1917, and Scott felt that the era of what he called bitter personal journalism died with him. His friendship with the new *Los Angeles Times* publisher Harry Chandler survived the battle with the general and proved lucrative in future fund-raising efforts for his various Catholic causes.

Recovering from his long-running dispute with Otis, Joseph was soon on his way to France at the behest of the Knights of Columbus, of which he was now a leading member, to organise welfare work for US soldiers at the war front. This was early 1918, but the German submarines did not catch up with his ship, as he put it, and he arrived safely in Paris. He was based for three months at a large military hospital near Paris and saw terrible scenes of suffering in the later stages of the conflict as United States servicemen joined French and British troops in the clash with the Kaiser's invaders. Joseph had a personal interest in the Great War: just before leaving California for France he learned that his 34-year-old brother Walter, who had joined the Canadian Army, had died in action.

Back home in Los Angeles in 1919 and ever the Irish nationalist, Scott found time to organise a major public rally, attended by over 15,000 people and featuring a 30-strong security contingent, for fugitive Republican leader Eamon de Valera, who had been spirited out of a troubled Ireland to his native New York as a stoker on a freighter.

The future President of the Irish Republic was just one of many celebrities who were welcomed to Los Angeles by Joseph Scott. He was chairman of the reception committee for the formal visit in 1922 of Marshal Ferdinand Foch, commander-in-chief of Allied Armies during World War I. He was chairman of the Lindbergh welcoming committee after the young aviator's historic solo flight across the Atlantic in 1927, and received Cardinal Pacelli, later to be Pope Pius XII. He met the legendary Irish tenor John McCormack and physicist Albert Einstein.

Although he never held significant elective office, Joseph Scott was an orator of dramatic power whose speeches were characterised by a transparent sincerity, spontaneous wit and exalted patriotism. At the Republican Party convention in Chicago in 1932 he was chosen to make the nomination speech for his fellow Californian Herbert Hoover for the presidency of the United States.

Years of public service and courtroom battles followed, none more famous than his 1945 paternity suit for 23-year-old starlet Joan Barry against Charlie Chaplin, in which he called the great comedian a lecherous swine, a master mechanic in the art of seduction, and a gray-headed old buzzard! Scott was 77 at the time and Chaplin 55. In a particularly dramatic courtroom scene, Scott held up his client's red-haired baby daughter and invited the jury to note the resemblance to Chaplin. There was no likeness but Scott won his case, despite blood tests seemingly exonerating Chaplin and evidence that Miss Barry had been stalking Chaplin – one night even entering his mansion with a gun, according to the butler – and seeing the multi-millionaire J. Paul Getty.

The 26-year-old Englishman with the Scots/Irish genes who stepped off the transcontinental train in Los Angeles that day in 1893 surely found his destiny when he threw himself into the legal profession. Any ordinary man would have been content to learn his trade before seeking to broaden his horizons, but this Penrith-born son of Joseph and Mary Scott would soon demonstrate his view of life's opportunities for service to his fellow man in countless ways, formal and informal, religious and secular. His vision and unfailing energy would win him papal honours five times by three

Old Plaza Church, Los Angeles, in the old Mexican quarter and below a wall plaque in memory of Joe Scott.

Popes, including Knight of St Gregory in 1920 for services during World War I. Two universities honoured him with prestigious medals as an outstanding lay Catholic, and the Holy Name Society gave him its Vercelli Medal in 1947. For many years dean emeritus of the Loyola Law School of Los Angeles, he was awarded honorary doctorates by four universities. As a Catholic layman, he made nationwide lecture tours and addressed International Eucharistic Congresses in Chicago, Budapest, Manila and Buenos Aires.

As early as May 1896, Scott was president of the Los Angeles Catholic Beneficial Association in aid of the sick and unemployed. He was actively involved with the Los Angeles Orphanage by 1898, in areas as diverse as arranging the children's music and consulting with the nuns on financial and legal matters, and in 1944 he was busy organising the orphanage's Advisory Board under the chairmanship of his son-in-law, J. Howard Ziemann, while establishing a reputation among the Sisters for always answering their letters the same day. Scott's concern to help the young was likewise evident in 1926, when he set up the Catholic Big Brothers in the Diocese of Los Angeles and San Diego for young people in trouble with the police and juvenile courts. He organised the Los Angeles Council of the Knights of Columbus in January 1902 – the year of that remarkable trip with his little son to Connecticut and onward to England – and was elected its first State Deputy.

If it is true that Joseph was best remembered for championing justice and freedom of conscience, his vigorous defence of a united Ireland was evidenced by his articulate leadership as president of the American League for an Undivided Ireland and as permanent chairman of the International Irish Congress. In San Francisco on 8 November 1953 he was honoured for his efforts on behalf of Irish freedom by people such as Cardinal James Francis McIntyre, Bishop Joseph T. McGucken, Governor Goodwin J. Knight, Los Angeles Police Chief W. A. Parker and Congressman Gordon McDonough. Principal speaker John Henning of San Francisco went so far as to draw a parallel between 86-year-old Scott's career and the story of the Irish struggle for independence.

Scott's determined support of humanitarian causes was not confined to the Irish cause. He gave assistance to Lithuanian refugees while at the same time promising his continued help to the Archbishop of China, the Most Reverend Thomas Tienchensin, when the archbishop appeared at the Los Angeles Breakfast Club in 1953 to solicit aid against Communist domination of his people.

One of his strongest denunciatory crusades against oppression was on behalf of the American Knights of Columbus when they pledged a million dollars to stamp out Communism in Mexico and the United States. At a Philadelphia meeting of the Knights on 5 August 1926, Chairman Scott told the 1,000 delegates they would be neglecting their duty if they failed to register their unqualified protest against the policy of President Calles of Mexico for his despotic use of armed force against his own people, who were struggling for the right to worship God according to the dictates of their conscience. His defence of the Polish people against Communism in the late 1940s earned him the title of honorary president of the Society for the Promotion of Polish Independence.

In 1894 a virulently anti-Catholic organisation calling itself the American Protective Association had gained a strong foothold in southern California with the express aim of excluding Catholics from public affairs and opposing them in business and the professions. Scott joined other Catholic laymen under Bishop George Montgomery in thwarting the tactics of the APA. An early public meeting in Los Angeles showed how strongly Republicans opposed the APA, and it was their stance against bigotry that decided Joseph where his political allegiance would lie. In similar vein, the Ku Klux Klan in southern California in the 1920s met forceful opposition under Scott's leadership, and the Knights of Columbus sent him into the southern states where he told the KKK 'to get out of their nightshirts if they were 100 per cent American!'

Going beyond mere opposition to bigotry against Catholics and other minority groups, Scott actually sought better inter-racial and inter-faith relations, to the extent that he could be considered an early promoter of ecumenism. Indeed, Scott was a founder of the Los Angeles Newman Club, which was sponsoring such activity as early as 1899. Likewise, in the early 1900s he was already emphasising the important role of Catholic laymen in the Church – a concept much stressed in mid-twentieth century Catholic ecclesiastical circles. Many years later, in 1946, when the National Conference of Christians and Jews was launched in Los Angeles, Scott was an original charter member of the Advisory Board, proving himself fearless in upholding what he deemed right even if at times his views were contrary to some higher authority.

Joseph was an active member of Catholic organisations like the Holy Name Society, whose objective was to help the poor and homeless, and in 1939 he founded the Nocturnal Adoration Society, remaining an active member for the rest of his life. This society required members to pledge themselves to spend an hour one night each month before the Blessed Sacrament at the Plaza Church of Our Lady Queen of the Angels in the city's old Mexican quarter. A wall plaque on the mission church of 1781 still has a bronze image of Joe Scott and a reference to him as district commander, Ronda Caravan No84, International Order of the Alhambra.

Such was Scott's stature in his adopted city that at the Civic Testimonial Dinner for his 84th birthday in 1951 he was referred to by a former mayor as 'First Citizen of Los Angeles.' He was always seen as a figure of great importance to the Republican Party. When US President Taft visited Los Angeles in 1909, Scott was principal speaker at his reception, and later on of course he was a staunch supporter of Herbert Hoover in his political ambitions at the highest level. Yet the only political office he held was a rel-

Colourful Characters of Cumbria's Eden Valley

11/97/37-1:

JOSEPH SCOTT LEO B. WARD J. HOWARD ZIEMANN CUTHBERT J. SCOTT A. H. RISSE G. L. McFARLAND	LAW OFFICES **JOSEPH SCOTT** 1001-1012 BLACK BUILDING 357 SOUTH HILL STREET LOS ANGELES, CALIFORNIA	PRIVATE EXCHANGE TRINITY 5361 CABLE ADDRESS "SCOTT LOS ANGELES" ADDRESS ALL COMMUNICATIONS TO JOSEPH SCOTT

July Ninth, 1940

Reverend Doctor Ed. Towers
Ushaw College
Durham, England

My dear Doctor Towers:

        Let me thank you for your profoundly interesting letter. It opens up a new vista of reflection and recollection -- particularly, the old Alma Mater housing a group of 140 officers after their gruelling experiences at Flanders and Dunkirk, is of itself an epochal event.

        The American press appears to treat the war as a news item of first magnitude; literally columns and pages daily being displayed for our information. The sympathy of the country generally, of course, is with the allies. The detestation for Hiterl grows apace, as his philosophy of life and governmental structure is abhorrent to the last degree to the American conception of law and order.

        I am very much interested in your quiet but none-the-less emphatic review of the spirit of the people and their confidence to withstand the shock of the Hitler invasion by air. I am telling my friends hereabouts that the coolness of you people under fire and under stress, whether in the storm at sea, or on the bloody battlefield, has been proverbial throughout the centuries. The numberless veterans of the old World War will give a good account of themselves in the Nazi parachute campaign against the "tight little Island".

        One thing it has done for this country-- it has bestirred them into the most lively pace of organizing themselves along preparedness defense lines. Hereabouts, as you may know, Southern California is one of the key-spots of the Nation in the aeroplane industry -- the big Douglas Aircraft Factory is working now twenty-four hours steadily -- and certainly you must have an enormous number of aeroplanes shipped to you folks over there. There are three other factories going full-blast likewise hereabouts.

        One of the things this war is doing for those who have little religious faith left -- it has put a big

Rev. Dr. Ed. Towers   -2-   July 9, 1940

interrogation point on some of our cynics and skeptics who are at their wits' end to know the solution of this terrific upheaval.

The Ushaw lads must certainly have an unusually keen appreciation of their responsibility, particularly those boys who are heading for the Lord's Vineyard must more than ever realize the "vanity of all earthly things."

Hereabouts, thank God, all goes well with us. George and Pat are active in their ecclesiastical duties and are in good health, and Al is giving a good account of himself on the bench. Cub is working with me steadily and improving his ability and resourcefulness daily.

Mrs. Scott is now the Grandmother of seven Grandchildren, and our youngest daughter, Josephine, is going to present her with another youngster in a couple of months. She is living over again the days of her young married life and, thank God, is in good health and strength.

As for myself, I am at this desk constantly. I will be 73 in a week's time and can't say that I feel the strain mentally or physically.

I received an amazingly long letter from my old friend, Father Joe Roche, whom we used to call "Cockroach" in our early days. He is now retired at Blackpool, but he is full of reminiscences of our Alma Mater as though he only left it yesterday.

Give my cordial regards and best wishes to the Right Reverend President and your colleagues in the parlor, and with affectionate greetings from Mrs. Scott and all the family, I am

Devotedly yours,

Joseph Scott

A letter to Ushaw College from Joseph Scott expressing his views as a Californian on aspects of World War II and he also mentions family matters.

atively minor one: he was elected to the Los Angeles School Board in December 1904, becoming its president three years later and serving in that capacity until 1915.

Appointment to the School Board was seen as essentially non-political, in furtherance of a policy of selecting non-partisan members without political affiliations. As early as 1910 apparently, a seat in the United States Senate was considered a possibility for Scott, but nothing came of it. At the Catholic Missionary Congress in Boston in 1913, where Scott was principal speaker, it emerged that the vice-chairman of the congress, the Very

Rev Dr Kelley, had been asked by US President Woodrow Wilson – perhaps rather pointedly – for the name of a Catholic lawyer living somewhere west of the Mississippi, a man of great ability who might be considered suitable for the United States Supreme Court. Dr Kelley said he did know of such a man (Joseph Scott), but he doubted if he would leave his beloved California even for so strong a temptation. Perhaps the fiery Scott would have seen political office as limiting his ability to speak freely on any subject that caught his attention.

Two highly prestigious posts this remarkable man was offered were hardly political but would certainly have taken him far from California. Would he become Governor General of the Philippines? Would he take the Governorship of Puerto Rico? No, he would not, was his firm response to both, although he appreciated the honour of being asked.

Nearer to home, around the same time as Joseph was on the Los Angeles School Board (1904-15), he was also a member of the city Chamber of Commerce – from 1907 to 1918, serving as president from 1910. This was a particularly challenging time for the Chamber, with its interest in great undertakings like the completion of the breakwater at San Pedro Harbour – a project in which Scott took a conspicuous part in dealing with problems of land acquisition – and the monumental 250-mile-long Owens River Aqueduct to bring desperately-needed water into the city from the Sierra Nevada Mountains.

Joseph Scott was prominent at various times on other Los Angeles bodies such as the Charter Revision Commission, Conference on Social Work and Community Chest. A Los Angeles humanitarian organisation that was founded in the difficult economic conditions of the later 1920s, the Community Chest was designed to bring most charitable groups and welfare agencies together into one powerful body for fundraising purposes. This cause was near to Joseph's heart, and he became its president in the distressing aftermath of the 1929 Wall Street crash as the Community Chest was swamped with cries for help from people facing unemployment, hunger and disease. He was deeply moved to be honoured in 1932 for his work with the Community Chest, with an award by the Los Angeles Realty Board and their designation of him as 'Los Angeles' Most Useful Citizen'. In 1933 he also served as chairman of Los Angeles County Emergency Relief Commission under the federal and state relief programme.

A founder member and trustee of the South West Museum, he was active in the Irish American Historical Society (awarded the society's medal in

Joseph Scott – Mr Los Angeles

Joseph Scott (centre) at Ushaw College at the age of 80 in 1948.

1948 for scholarly contributions) and an official of many southern California athletic, social and historical clubs and societies. He became chairman of the Los Angeles Boys Week committee in 1931; chairman of the Citizens Committee for the Army and Navy; director, United Service Organisations, Los Angeles War Chest. As Hon vice-president, Panama Pacific International Exposition, San Francisco 1915, he was appointed by President Hoover to the George Washington Bicentennial Commission, 1932, and was a member of the Los Angeles, California and American Bar Associations. His Catholic clubs were California, Newman, Sunset (president 1923-24), and he was a member of the Los Angeles and Pasadena Athletic Clubs. He served as Chairman of the District Draft Board, southern California 1917-1918, and he was special commissioner for the Knights of Columbus in France and England in 1918.

Joseph's 90th birthday celebration at the Biltmore Hotel in Los Angeles on 16 July 1957 was attended by 900 people. Anyone who contemplates the range of activities he crammed into his long life must wonder how even 90 years could possibly have been enough to do it all. Yet above all he was a family man who insisted that he reserved weekends for his children, a man who in his eighties could look back on 'those Sundays 45 and 50 years ago when we'd get up early for Mass, breakfast and get our lunches packed. Mother stayed home to rest. She needed it after the week. This was my day with the children. The older ones each had a bike and had them ready for the road. I tossed the little ones in the back of the surrey, hitched up Babe the horse, and off we went to the beach.'

Joe Scott was a great American. He died of pneumonia in hospital on 24 March 1958, ten days after a fall in his law office. Four days later, the US House of Representatives heard a glowing tribute to him in which it was said that 'a rich chapter in the history of Los Angeles has been completed with the death of Joseph Scott. It would be difficult to say whether the growth of this great city paralleled the life of Joseph Scott or vice versa. Probably to say both would better serve the truth.'

He was survived by his wife Bertha and their three sons and three daughters, with 23 grandchildren. His body lay in state at the City Hall, and at his funeral in St Vibiana's Cathedral his son Mgr. George Scott sang the solemn requiem in the presence of the Cardinal Archbishop. The bishop of Sacramento preached the sermon and five other Californian bishops were there, together with many priests and around 2,000 friends. Ireland's ambassador to Washington represented his country's president, and official condolences were issued by US Vice-President Nixon.

Joseph Scott was regarded as Ushaw College's best known layman. Despite remembering the college's Spartan regime in terms of 'blue milk and east wind', his abiding loyalty to Ushaw was evident in his speech at the 1908 centenary and also in 1948, when he flew from Los Angeles at the age of 80 for the college's Grand Week. He was at Ushaw in September 1913 to enrol his three sons Cuthbert aged eight, George, ten, and Alfonso, eleven. His Irish mother Mary, whose 'indomitable Catholic spirit and uncompromising heart' had ever been his guiding light, died in nearby Darlington on 15 December 1913, six years after his father Joseph.

Joe Scott never tired of recalling his birthplace at Penrith in 'that most beautiful corner of England, about five miles from Lake Ullswater.'

Washington Family in Westmorland
And the Virginian who nearly went to Appleby Grammar School

George Washington was a fifteen-year-old surveyor working on the Fairfax estates by the Potomac river in Virginia in 1747. But for a twist of fate still fresh in his mind, the future first President of the United States of America would have been at school four thousand miles away in England, like his late father Augustine had been – and his two half-brothers and an uncle.

Destined to be immortalised as 'Father of his Country', George Washington would always regret his lack of an English education. Under his inspirational leadership in war and peace, the original thirteen colonies of America would become an independent nation whose territory extended from the Atlantic coast to the Mississippi River, while he conferred on the presidency a prestige so great that American political leaders ever afterwards would deem it the highest distinction to occupy the chair he honoured between 1789 and 1797.

The genealogists take us back to Walter de Wessyngton, an Englishman who fought with Henry III at the Battle of Lewes in 1264, and trace the great George Washington's lineage to Walter's youngest son John and his wife Elizabeth, heiress of Gilbert de Burneside of Burneside Hall near Kendal (while another son, Robert, married into the lordly Strickland family of nearby Sizergh Castle).

The transatlantic story comes into focus with Royalist clergyman's son John Washington, who left England for Virginia in the aftermath of the Civil War and carved out for himself a sizeable estate in the east of the growing colony. His son and heir, Col Lawrence Washington, was a leading tobacco planter who died in 1698, leaving a widow, Mildred, with two small sons, John and Augustine, and an infant daughter, Mildred. That untimely event was a foretaste of trials in store, as a stalwart colonial family paved the way for emergence in adversity many years later, of the most illustrious Washington of all. It was also the start of a train of events that would lead from Virginia's Westmoreland to the old county of Westmorland in England.

The Virginia tobacco crop was the preserve of merchants from English ports, with Whitehaven in Cumberland at the forefront of the lucrative trade and canny Cumbrian brothers George and Matthias Gale among its leading exponents.

George Gale, 28-year-old master of the 200-ton *Cumberland*, dropped anchor in Virginia's Rappahannock River in January 1700. By the middle of May the enterprising young captain had loaded his cargo of tobacco and married well-to-do widow Mildred Washington, before joining a convoy of at least a dozen vessels and heading out into the Atlantic with his new wife and three children by her first marriage, plus a coloured servant Jane.

The good ship *Cumberland* made landfall in bustling Whitehaven, but the Washington family who had survived their weeks under sail had barely settled into their new home by the Irish Sea when they were beset by tragedy. Poor Mildred died soon after the birth of a child in January 1701, to be followed to her grave in the town's St Nicholas's churchyard by her servant in February, and a baby daughter in May.

George Gale became legal guardian of the three Washington children, as his wife Mildred had wished, and entered John and Augustine as boarders at Appleby Grammar School, which was a flourishing establishment of high repute. Gale, though, eventually lost custody of the children in a Virginia court, and around Christmas 1703 young John and Augustine said their farewells to Appleby, for return with their sister Mildred to their uncle John on the other side of the Atlantic.

Augustine Washington was a successful colonial businessman in his 30s when he visited England in 1729 and installed his eleven-year-old son Lawrence at his old school at Appleby. Three years later the energetic Virginian brought his younger son, Austin, over to the renowned Eden seat of learning, and the Washington brothers each spent some nine years at the school under celebrated headmaster Richard Yates, who thought highly of them both.

No stranger to family disaster, Augustine Washington lost his 30-year-old wife Jane while he was away in 1729 on that trip to England with his eldest son Lawrence, and back in Virginia he married 24-year-old Mary Ball, who became the mother of George Washington early in 1732.

Young George was destined to follow his older half-brothers to the far-off English school that had left such an abiding impression on his father and uncle, but the ill-starred Washingtons were dealt yet another blow when Augustine died suddenly in 1743, aged 49. George was then eleven years old and his strong-willed mother insisted on keeping him at home in Virginia with his five younger brothers and sisters.

Steeled in British battles against the French in his homeland and irked by colonial iniquity, George Washington was animated by the ideal of creating a nation dedicated to the rights of man, and his success in that endeavour put him in the first rank among figures of world history. While he may have regretted his lack of an English schooling, he did learn much from his Appleby-educated half-brothers, especially the cultured Lawrence who had continued to correspond for a number of years with his old headmaster, Richard Yates.

The 'Peacracker' lives on
The search for a veteran motorcycle

Ravenglass in the 1950s watched over its three rivers just as Roman Glannaventa had done near two millennia before. Long gone now were the far-flung Empire's menacing galleys, like the sailing ships and the shadowy smugglers of old; and just about all that was left of the ancient village's proud seafaring tradition was the battered rowing boat in which wily factotum Jack Pharaoh would ferry gullible visitors over to the gulleries in the sand dunes across the bay.

Wartime food rationing was fresh in villagers' minds and four-legged horsepower was still in action on the broad main street. Car ownership was but a dream for most folk, even with change out of a £1 for four gallons of petrol, although one aspiring young Lothario with a bob or two to spare strutted his stuff in a trendy black Ford 'Pop', no less, while the diminutive Rev M. K. Hodges MA (Cantab) raised parishioners' eyebrows on his thumping great 350 AJS motorbike.

Then there was the 'Peacracker'. The old Velocette two-stroke with the staccato soundtrack and early Cumberland number plate 'RM 151' had first flexed its muscles at John Fletcher Stout's Egremont cycle shop way back in 1924. Now into its fourth decade as trusty transport, the quaint little bike with the footboards and outside flywheel would often excite the youth of the quiet seaside village and linger in the memory of one comely maid long after her uncle, John Cornthwaite from Wasdale, parted with it in 1959 after thirteen years of careful ownership.

The austere 50s were giving way to the swinging 60s when 'RM 151' moved north to Distington near Whitehaven, where impecunious but discerning young engineer Ken Severs put a few more miles under its wheels before parting with it for £5. Ken was happy with his fiver because that was what he had paid John Cornthwaite.

The rest of the twentieth century had melted away, along with a bit of the twenty-first, when the aforementioned young lady from 50s Ravenglass fondly recalled her late uncle's distinctive old bike, the 'Peacracker', and

The 'Peacracker' lives on

wondered whether it had survived the ravages of time.

Believing it had gone to a museum in the Penrith area, the winsome grandmother enlisted the help of the writer. But the bottom line was that the spluttering two-stroke's trademark haze of exhaust smoke was last seen at Distington in 1961.

Manfully suppressing dark thoughts of that near half-century void and the inevitable scrapyard, the Eden Valley historian with more of a track record for finding adventurous local people than long-lost antiques had a depressingly short list of 'possibles' when he rang old-established Rowgate Garage at the Eden Valley town of Kirkby Stephen. He had barely introduced himself and got as far as 'RM...' when the helpful voice on the other end broke in with '...151!'

For 46 years the venerable Velocette had been hiding away in a disused car showroom at Kirkby Stephen among veteran cars and motorcycles hoarded in the 'Genevieve' era by far-sighted garage owner Tom Potter. Still sporting its original livery and a long-expired excise licence, the old bike had been kept by the enthusiastic collector and then by his family of three sons and a daughter just as it was when it was brought across the county from Distington all those years ago.

As luck would have it, 'RM 151' had not been among the veterans that left the second-generation Potters' time-warp premises at sales they held after their enterprising father, Tom, died in 1974. An ancient product of a long-gone Birmingham factory, it had survived against all the odds to resurface around 80 miles from the place where its original proud owner first prodded its modest motor into life. It was enough to bring a lump to a crusty old historian's throat.

But the 'Peacracker's' long-term custodians at Kirkby Stephen were nearing retirement and already thinking about parting with their inherited collection of veteran vehicles. Looking a bit forlorn (or maybe just coy about that £5 deal in 1961), the worthy runabout duly took the stand at an important Harrogate sale just a few months later.

International auctioneers Bonhams recognised the remarkably well preserved little Velocette as something of a rarity and valued it at £3,000 to £4,000. Bidding was brisk and the hammer soon came down at £6,200 to send old Cumbrian 'RM 151' on its way to a collector in the Channel Islands.

Colourful Characters of Cumbria's Eden Valley

By the same author

John Metcalfe Carleton: Georgian Rake of the Eden Valley

The Workman Brothers: English Pioneers of the American West
(shortlisted for the 2014 Lake District Book of the Year Award)

About the Author

JOHN SHARPE studied Classics at Durham University and followed National Service in the Army with a working life in the police. A native of Cumbria, he has lived in the county's Eden Valley since the 1960s. His speciality as a biographer is the unsung hero – or villain. The Eden Valley is a rich mine of worthy material.

Colourful Characters of Cumbria's Eden Valley